MASCULINITY:

AN ANTHOLOGY OF MO

Rick Dove is a progressive poet and activist from South West London. Published widely in anthologies and journals since 2016, and dubbed "one to watch" by TS Eliot Prize winner Roger Robinson, Rick also has two full collections with Burning Eye Books, *Tales From the Other Box* (August 2020), and *Supervillain Origin Story* (May 2023). Rick has performed across the UK and internationally and was crowned Hammer & Tongue UK Poetry Slam Champion in 2021.

Aaron Kent is a working-class writer, stroke survivor, and insomniac from Cornwall. His 2nd collection, *The Working Classic*, is available from the87press. He has read his poetry for The BBC, The Shakespeare Birthplace Trust, and Stroke Association, had work published in various journals, and is an Arvon tutor. His poetry has been translated into languages including French, Hungarian, German, Cymraeg, and Kernewek, and has been set to music.

Stuart McPherson is a prize-winning poet from the UK. His poems have appeared in *Butcher's Dog Magazine, Bath Magg, Poetry Wales, Anthropocene, Blackbox Manifold, Prelude* and *One Hand Clapping*. In October 2022, Stuart was the winner of the Ambit Annual Poetry Competition. His second collection, *End Ceremonies,* was published via Broken Sleep Books on August 31st 2023.

B EQUALITY YOND

RETHINK MASCULINITIES

BEYOND EQUALITY works to engage men in a brave and transformative rethinking of what 'being a man' means for them and others. Through workshops in schools, universities, workplaces, and other sites, we give people the opportunity to make a difference to issues that matter to them. We believe men can and must play a role in undoing the violence of sexism and patriarchy, and help to build a world based on respectful, positive, and equitable relationships.

www.beyondequality.org

Masculinity:
An anthology of modern voices

Edited by
Rick Dove, Aaron Kent, and Stuart McPherson

Broken Sleep Books

ISBN: 978-1-915760-87-6

The author has asserted their right to be identified as the author of this Work in accordance with the Copyright, Designs and Patents Act 1988

Cover designed by Aaron Kent and Joseph Kent

Edited by: Rick Dove, Aaron Kent, and Stuart McPherson

Typeset by Aaron Kent

Broken Sleep Books Ltd
Rhydwen
Talgarreg
Ceredigion
SA44 4HB

Broken Sleep Books Ltd
Fair View
St Georges Road
Cornwall
PL26 7YH

Contents

FOREWORD

Since starting my artistic career, this project is the one that I spent the least time deciding on whether or not I wanted to be a part of or not. For me, masculinity is in need of a new narrative, an empathetic and emotionally open, and vulnerable narrative, that embraces the multitudes of manhood and what that might mean in a non-toxic future, and that abandons the unreconstructed and restrictive definitions that have gone before. A chance to contribute to that, in even a small way, was too good an opportunity to turn down.

The call went out, and the quality of the work submitted was genuinely stunning, it seems that many poets writing today, felt the same as we did, and selecting pieces from the hundreds received was a Herculean task. I am incredibly grateful and thankful to Aaron and Stuart for allowing me to be part of this team and it was heartening to see how closely we marked pieces (No favourites will be named, I realise now that being an editor is very much like being a parent, no favourites...). Contributors, I love you all, thank you for trusting us with your work.

— Rick Dove

Recently I was at the school for the school run when the class teacher did the dreaded thing of summoning a parent over, meaning we all knew that parent's child had misbehaved to some extent. The naughty kid's mum came back from the conversation to explain to her friend that her 5-year-old son had been chasing the girls in his class in an attempt to kiss them, and did not stop when they asked him to. Her friend cheerily stated 'oh, boys will be boys.' This line of thought, still prevalent in modern society, leads to a culture where toxic masculinity is accepted and excused under the guise that we know no better.

This book was important to me as an attempt to counter that mindset, as proof that masculinity is not a one-size-fits-all construct. It has taken me years to be able to fully express emotion, and to share that emotion with other men, but now, to be in a book where masculinity is presented as a gourmet of forms, rather than a dominant idea, means I am held within the pages herewith. To have worked with both Rick and Stuart to create this remarkable book, and to present masculinity through such diverse lenses, is a real highlight of mine, and proof of a progressive, considerate, emotive masculinity.

Boys might be boys, but boys can certainly be better.

— Aaron Kent

The words 'Man', 'Men', and 'Masculinity' are three very complicated ideas for me. I say *ideas* because in terms of definition, it seems very difficult to pin down exactly what these things mean. What *is* masculinity? And what does being a man actually entail? As a default, there seems to be a commonly held mental image bound to a particular construct of men, as nature's aggressors, as unemotional animals who fight, fuck, and bring home food for the family; a survival of the fittest where only the strongest survive. Whilst this may be apparent in some instances, is it always true?

So the question really becomes *why* does this exist? For patriarchal control? For capitalism? For the monetization of combat sports? I don't have the answer, but what I *do* know is that I have never identified with it. I'm emotional, I'm scared by the world, I appreciate tenderness, and I've never felt comfortable joining in when other men are beating their chests in public. I also believe that these feelings are commonly held, but often hidden from view, which, as we know, is a real problem for both mental and physical health.

This is where expression becomes crucial and is why *this* anthology is crucial. Without expression, without voice, discussion and deconstruction is impossible. Without discussion nothing changes, and in this instance, toxic ideas of masculinity continue to prevail. I'm proud to have been able to read and absorb all of the words contained within this book. It is a wholesome and honest account of feeling. I hope you enjoy it too, and I hope it provokes some interesting thoughts along the way.

— Stuart McPherson

spit & sawdust

Boxing gloves come as standard in blue and red.
You wrap your hands first — my favourite part.
Hand wrapping is an art in itself—
rolling the wraps, after they've been washed
each week, is a form of meditation.
Once your hands are wrapped and you have warmed up
you work your fighting hands into each glove,
push down, Coach pulls the gloves up, one by one,
the sound of velcro closing on your wrists.
But some people say boxing is violent.
I remember hitting only heavy bags
on my light feet, afterwards shaking, as
cuss words echoed in the rafters like birds.

a spinning top, maybe

a
-kindly-
kind-of-ener
gy-can-lift-a-car-a
-finger-run-into-a-burn
ing-building-blocks-hung
over-no-doubt-winning-fa
ther-of-the-crawl-across-a-
mad-expanse-of-carpet-til
ing-vomit-garden-insects
-trapped-beneath-toy-
car-in-flames-a-su
per-human-sup
er-strength-
drunk-on
-paren
tal-
lo
v
e

meantime

johnny boy makes nice with his city humor
                                        by bewildering
                cocked & loaded wise-guy

        bomb in the mailbox
                                a desire to break attention

        luckyunlucky   bones & clams
                                    black & white
                                    strippers & wanderers
        night judgment   to drink & walk
                                    ducking debts
                                                        undone

                with drug   appointed
        drudge
                        of his flock
                                        contagious psyche swigging him
                & jimmy
                        & tony
                                & charlie
                                        & michael
                & joey

                                                naturally johnny
                        boy's the greasy
                foil

            charlie's negative charge

        slipped between
                        mafioso
                petit bourgeois
        & arioso   petty
        bullshit

        a mess of codes
                    agog to cross
                            their hearts their
                                        hearts
                            their

                    streets
            burn cold against
                    the radio's   activities

        loverboys* with butterflies
                                    jerk-off opulence
            cupping   half wingéd   saviors

        hot air cradling
                catching   &
        pushing them

                            through a
                            mammalian
                            season
                            of glory

        in   the blazing fallout   of the moon
                shadows'   pooling   rhythms—

        circadian   scattershot

---

*

Scene Wakes (to be you)

if you're Jimmy
- keep your mouth shut   ■ joey? how come?
- I'm a mook?   ■ you can't call me a mook

if you're Joey
- pulsing trouble   ■ eager to plume, a feathered ogre
- what's a matter with this guy?   ■ alright   ■ we're not paying
- we're not gonna pay   ■ we're not paying cuz' this guy
- this guy's a fuckin' mook   ■ we don't pay mooks

if you're Johnny Boy
- day walking into a bar   ■ smiling at joey's cheap sneakers
- being fresh & pretty   ■ youcallthoseskanksgirls?
- you tell me that in front thiz ass-ole?   ■ amookwhat'samook?

If you're liquored & a debt pressed
- threshold of honor is threshed   ■ renege
- find egress under the bar   ■ erase

if you're The Marvelettes
- Wait!   ■ Oh yes wait a minute Mr. Postman
- Wait!   ■ Way-ay-ay-ait Mr. Postman

wound them

up to drum;

nobody's got

a gun   a cop   gets to Jersey
        &   to Philly

                                        with a pocketknife   & a song

                                subatomic   laws making light

                        thin

sticky skin
                        of little
                                        italy convulsing
                                                        in ultraviolent
        harmony

multiplicity   of the unchanging brain's   opaque

eyeballs   amassing   wherever   there is decay

i've got the music in me

mawkish denomination
eating soap like its the true

        fruit - ethnicity cleansed
        by heroic labors - levitation

desired of genetic signatures &
splinters gather in my fingers—

        cupid's arrows nocking wingéd
        behaviors - subatomic & immutable

bylaws of the night's bright
milk light do not care about

        my evil twins, my secret children,
        my chatty neighbors, my secondary

plotlines or my second bananas
in the scrap metal bent for

        long-term endgames & enclosures
        whose the most devoted to the straightest

talks by the straightest talkers?
slipped in the slime mold

        of radio's baby beast
        it's an open system, it's uncontained

it's typical, it's a masque of gold
sloughed civility & here i am

        the angst supposed
        the fish eager to be fished

the bird glancing at its fossils
the fly's faith in the frog spit

        yet the maw's aria of influence wails
        faith - sunday white to raise

the dead - how bizarre, a bucket hat
newly radicalized - elemental

        pandemonium every time i
        muck around it's in my face

losing our minds
don't give up

losing our sight
don't let go

the clown's are stuck
but i'm comin' home

i'm faster than a muddy ferret
more powerful than a criminal motive

able to lilt old yearlings with
a single sound - a mook

up in the sky - a bird again
i'm super maneuverable - so give

it to me now - flat & sharp to
get the music out - a fluid

& devout detergent's smaller
part of a bloody century - something

washed - something blue
something light - mister butterfly

noise of water - love of floating
basic reflux of air's breathing

Sports Bar

Artificial light glints
from his skinhead head –
chiselled with work ethic
strengthened with exhaust fumes
and polished with Stella.

His coat is blacker
and his jeans are less blue.
The team that's his is better
and the brand his money floats
is more desirable.

His relationship with his mother
is just as deep as yours
and he longs for his father's approval.
He prays daily for his child's safety
and his fear is just as real.

If you get in his way
he will laugh with his friends
until you feel as small as you are
compared to all of them.
Shrinking
you will show your vulnerability.

His is tucked away in a secret drawer
with a milk tooth
a love letter
and a lock of hair.

He grips your side
as he slides by,
the intimacy sanctioned
by a code as old
as his grandad's grandad's schoolteacher.

He catches your eye
winks.
The last act in a performance
before his beer takes centre stage once again.

Pattern for a Man

Begin with a scrap of sky blue
poplin cotton one inch squared.
Pin to the left shoulder of a man,
early 30s, as he steps from the
final train to return to his wife
and two boys, not yet in school.
Pin another each time he
completes his commute. Add
round white buttons, squared
edges, plastic. White thread.
Stitch cuffs inch by inch, then
collar. Synch with a silk tie one
stripe at a time.

Begin with a roll of African wax
print cotton. Sky blue, satsuma
orange, veins of red – the kind
of pattern that hangs on the
retina. Drape as he steps from
the plane to meet his partner's
family before the wedding.
When he comes next year sew
two short sleeves. Hem with
thread that brings out his eyes.
When he arrives, worrying
for the safety of the freighted
furniture, fix a single mother of
pearl button, though he'll never
use it.

All His Dreams on VHS

The day dad died we found all his dreams on VHS,
immaculately labelled and catalogued A–Z in a box
under the bed.

From **A**:	*At Night When Rivers Sleep*
to **B**:	*Belly Slit with Bowie Knife*
through **K**:	*Knights at the Circus*
P:	*Preacher & Cyanide*[†]
and **Z**:	*Zorbing in the Nude*

[†] In perfect Technicolor™ glitch, the dream begins:

It's clear that there are various ways into the hall
of mirrors but no way out,
and they are coming at me thick and fast,
unbidden thoughts and unwanted feelings like
river ghosts fleeing an old dry dock. Hands pulling
the skin at your hips—this naked image of you in
the mirror remains, skeletal, haunting the tain.

A quick pint of Olde Immortal Light in the
Preacher & Cyanide will set it right, right? It feels
like the long walk-of-shame home, and this
plangent hop-song an insect-like echo trapped in a
cathedral of spiders: from the antiphon 'Ghost
wife, come home ... come home ... come home'
to the homily 'Descend the path
no more ... no more ... no more'.

Now the cracks in the mirror are fissures between fiction and reality, the memory riven. The past, only the shell of a burnt-out tower block, a castle of mirrors through which your ghost once stepped. This light's slow dip to darkness is made of heterotopia, grey floodplains that reflect time's infinite regress.

Words laid down in replica, like light-waves skimming the surface: confessions whispered at the ocean's edge.

Melancholy III
after Edvard Munch (1902)

Despondent, he sits crushed by the weight of the lovers' tryst,
Oda's skin a blushed post-coital pink beneath wind-washed dress.
Bathed in the forlorn blue-grey light of Nordic summer nights,
Åsgårdstrand sinks deeper into rust, brindling with longing.
This fretsawed life, our atoms shuddering into being, and always
a maddening, muffled sadness skying up, inking our days.

He dreams of a song sung by his unborn, a suffocation of dusk,
the drift and dead light to the north, the fjord's river-gravel roan.
He becomes stone, darkening at the edges, the lovers departed,
her afterglow pouring up through him, a frozen smoke of grief.
Under the mask of a drowned man a face rains away to leave only
till-filled eyes and unkissed lips that whisper the way to nothing.

accusative masculine singular

"y'cunky!" - an affectation of affectionate **vernac** faux-Glaswegian from the nominal, nomative, gliss-gobbed gobby **volly** of sluicy, sauced up pals in a pissed-up pal-*athon.*

a normative lewd gob-off re-born in matey, libatey, backslap **churn**; incubated in the radicatorium of a bar-room's studiously **sham** brawlings and the display mode pepper-spray

of bonding, binding curse/**cuss** words in free-fall clashcade herding a tether of barking guffawers to the **trough** of taps and optics and a pissed, fug-fuddled, cursory squizz

at their lives collectively to come of 'making do', in which these self-professed, **pedestrian**, *"fukkin' mad"* moments will be the memories, possessing all too readily, too wholly

and all the more, all too **sadly** sorely, **hung** on to...

Bestiary of the Jaguar

In the photograph, the President kneels beside it. With one hand he
holds a rifle. With the other he supports its head. It is not asleep. It is not
dreaming. It is a sphinx in awkward repose, no longer poised, no longer
painted on some child's nursery wall. This is savagery incarnate, under the
guise of conservation. The underside of one paw is exposed to the camera.
Eyes closed, yet teeth exposed, as though being made to smile at its own
fate, to participate in this staging of manhood, to take it and take it and
take it and say *Yes, Sir. Thank you, Sir. Thank you, Mr President.* And all the
while, rosettes bloom and multiply, each the smudge of a hawk roosting
at the apex of the forest trees, each a bird in a row of birds on a power
line in a polyglot city of no love, each an oil spill within the fabrications
of industry, each a cell generating more cells, each a kernel of generations
who have fallen prey and will yet fall prey to this man, who once boasted
of going on a safari and killing nine lions, eight elephants, seven giraffes,
three pythons, two ibises and a crocodile. "It made our veins thrill",
he wrote, this colonel, who, in the photograph, is a smudge of white
moustache and spectacles, the entire earth a face looking upward for his
inspection, the whole of Creation reduced to this: no sophistry in his body,
whose one path is direct through the bones of the living. No argument
defies his right, the sun is behind him. A year before the Brazilian trip,
Nijinsky becomes a faun.

Bestiary of the River of Doubt

The photograph was taken by the President's son. Kermit, as a child, was sickly but had a flair for language and reading. As a freshman, he accompanied his father on a year-long expedition in Africa. For another expedition, to South America, he delayed his marriage. Like his father, he contracted malaria on the trip. But evidence suggests that he downplayed his illness to save medicine for his father's use. There is a picture of Kermit in the Amazon with a beard and a hat, his eyes knowing and silent, but mainly silent. There is a picture, too, from years earlier of him holding his dog Jack, who looks at some force in the distance, as the ochre light of late afternoon cries on the scene. Although partridges steal one another's eggs, Leonardo Da Vinci wrote, the young, when they have been hatched, always return to their true parents. When Kermit died in Alaska he never knew if he pleased his father.

The deer and the hunters

Bound away—
from the tread of boots,
the spoor of empty beer cans.

Leap creek and fern
to a maze of boulders.

Mist swabs
a burr-grazed flank.

Now there's rain.

Below they have tired, they
return to their masculine cars...

Rev of engines.
The convoy slurs down the hill.
The meagre lights of town.

F & B Used Cars, Swan Street, Richmond

Finch was often, even before noon, tired,
napped on the office sofa.
Twenty minutes horizontal restored him.

Bolster smoked too many Benson & Hedges,
his knees hurt.

Men and women passed the car yard
on E-bikes, skateboards, or with their $4000 dogs.

Bolster stood back from the dartboard,
which hung from a nail on the back wall,
to the left of a Pirelli Tyres poster.
Two of the darts landed short,
one punctured a half-deflated Christmas balloon.

Finch had been to Pirelli Headquarters in Milan or so he'd claimed.
Bolster remained sceptical. In thirty years, he'd never seen Finch
order an espresso or have a slice of pizza. And when pressed
Finch couldn't name a single Milanese football team...
but lies, embellishment, flattery, flirtation, fast and smooth talk,
all sold cars.

Here was a guy now, walking into the yard. Could have dressed better.
Could take his hands out of his pockets...
The world was full of timewasters and Bolster knew it,
as he butted out his cigarette in an ashtray.
And walked out into the afternoon heat,
tried to raise a smile.

a gesture of acknowledgement

the penrose step of being both one up and down, first brown, then man enough to understand exactly what it took to be a lover: the trick of rule, the cunning of a fool who runs his empty lines until he spies a chance to soothe his fear of missing out, his vapid sense of scarcity, of having been excluded from some grand arena. the dousing of a febrile need to be let in, to assert a sense of self. we smudge the fine print at the bottom of the page and cross the contract blindly. a season of goodwill to every man of violence, whose claim to the throne lies with the stone inside his heart, the granite affirmation of his wealth, his plastic health and empty cheer, his central state forever self-confirming. we master proof of rank to claim the badge devout. we give it all to make the kill, to find ourselves contorted on the floor, beneath ourselves. we catch those hands but dial it up and beat it on again. this is the father tongue. we fall before that swollen bone for some relief from our own obstruction. we seek a hole to fill, according to instruction, to kill the feeling worthless. the triumph of one inside the other is in the boot held tight against a neck that can never be let go. there is no sovereign without subject underfoot. we're held this way in the constant tension of position: in a frozen study of revenge, in punishment for all, caught in the act of always jumping ship, ablaze in rage, while still, below, remaining locked up in the hold.

for men, foment, fo' Moten

we get grown without a care by brittle looks that covet every throne
presaging naked estrangement, aligning with the undoubtable cop out
of each good man's loathe to hurt you, still you're out walking in dread,
looking back in increments, the message unfolding on your lap, how we
plan to lay siege, balling like our papas, the balling stance of papa and his
coveted disqualifier, the task he left us with his sword, the role that leaves
us bloody and departed. we know the ones our gaze sees feel what it is to
be stepped on, still tighten up their triple exploitation. the timing works
to keep us all in play here. the reflux word of always to abscond leaves us
narcissistic and collateral. we discharge what we do not repress, in urinal
and in knife. we stan the tycoon as epoch insulant, mold his perversities
as a buddy in amusement at frailty; we suffer all our brittle walls alone
stocked with funny quotes, stay biding time inside our tantrums and our
morning yawns, all conforming and in tall huddles; this alone career is the
worst of our command to part. all the sons who can't get over, hunched
again bereft while reeling from this man game, our brittle walls holding
the jewel of our mourning delayed, till the wealth reflects past their
persuasion, past the rift and snide of each hack buddy and his tune of gas,
in a hearse alone at last without a care, no longer loving warfare, no longer
breaking stones to distract our buddies from their brittle walls, their welds
and cataracts, the better to see a son's lack of heartfelt play, mistaken,
spewed back in gas and forced evasion, waving, going anyway, with
treason everywhere, just care for duels and unfathomably gunning down
every man least of heft till he is grown mute: the renowned confirmation
of the man role, all locked up in contracting praxis, in layers of the game
called grab her and gatherer, in walls and walls all surrounded by bluffers,
surrounded by the brawling stance, by long bodies hung and butchered
on the wall, the spoils of war, your vocal weaponry burning up beloved
chattel, your knife wounds beneath the tears of all the quiet folk bent on
weaving through this endless gauntlet with resolve.

Fitter Happier

recycle diligently>>>weight loss journey>>>check pension balance>>>
use caffeine shampoo>>>go wild swimming>>>sign online petitions>>>
see bands from your youth>>>retro trainers>>>create a compost heap>>>
self-diagnose medical conditions>>>learn to ride a big motorbike>>>
daily trips to the tip>>>wax body parts>>>eat high fibre breakfast cereal>>>
shave with a cut-throat razor>>>try coasteering>>>no means no>>>
build a vinyl collection>>>learn to homebrew>>>get a caravan>>>
go to middle class music festivals>>>before and after>>>cycle in lycra>>>
drink artisanal IPA>>>electric scooter>>>run 10k every day>>>hair loss treatment>>>
drive a campervan>>>amazing results>>>learn a language>>>take up golf>>>
paddleboard>>>sack, back and crack>>>grow a beard>>>buy unnecessary power tools>>>
keep tabs on your share prices>>>get a Tesla>>>it's good to talk>>>wear a Fitbit>>>
when the fun stops, stop>>>

My Way

His son helps him up to the microphone,
the shuffle and stiff smile we've seen all week.

A big family group, fifteen or so,
proud of him and their nan/mum.

The backing track starts and the grin is gone,
the fog clears and he begins to perform.

We forget about the heat, swatting mosquitoes,
turn in our plastic chairs to watch.

The voice may tremble slightly, but at its core
there is undeniable strength and polish.

Now, this is not a pool bar in Greece,
we aren't tourists drinking all-inclusive;

he's back on the cabaret circuit, gigging
from club to club, PA system in the van.

Begins to work us, a wink here, grin there,
throws the mic from one hand to the other.

We're on our feet as the song reaches its peak,
clap and whistle, wave phone torches.

He bows, the family surround him, give hugs,
grateful for a glimpse of the man they know.

digressed

Go into powder, and go
into the blue with your arms

into gear. Pad about, or pretend
to row, or grope for apricots

behind the scrim. Such a match
in peroxide can make up your

difference and his, your partner
weirdo. You are wired for another,

sure, and so many dents in kits and
tresses run shaking for varnish,

and the dusty companies go clean
in their one step. Part in waves. Look

dazzling in a fresh portmanteau
while I bring myself, harsh, to your

two smooth sides. I'll liken myself
to the worse and worsening tear

in this huge folly. I am awake
to the bluff, to the thousand petty

cuts that will be the cup of feeling.
And I'm willing to sport it, like bones

for bread, now as the bird bobs once,
and is roused to bleach the screen.

Flowery

i.m. Roddy Lumsden

The skies are humble already, and the swims
we take are the next frontier in diplomatic
crises. We're already fasting from steak,

halloumi the way we like it, going to town,
in advance of slipping our appetite for them.
Crazy all these years, let's make the years

a new kind of hold, a one weird gap reliable –
like your obligation to step aside on platforms,
to slot one's elegy in. We are in here with you

aren't we? Brush yourself down, take Lucozade for
tears, love them anon, and go skating under the sun.

The Cosmological Principle States That There are no Fixed Points, and Therefore They Cannot Move (But I am and I Do)

mostly i am tired of not healing   as you sit over me in the bath wash my hair
i am limp and thinking about forgiveness   what it means to forgive   i have
to weigh up what they know   your slim fingers full of organic shampoo
force their way   into my scalp and i sigh   mutter these lines   i am tired of
not healing   push with my little   strength back into your hands which are
small and unforgettable   so much so i wish i'd have known them   first but
your son i do not let him see me sad   not if i can help it   i will be the fixed
point for you both and i'm tired of not healing and i think about forgiveness
about my father's drunk red fists in the peat   and palms on the cheeks of
sad lovers   i think about forgiveness and remember your hands in my hair
Rebecca you ask me to pass you the jug which has sunk   and rinse away the
suds like i am your child   but i remember i am not   and i remember
that you are pregnant and the swollen joy of this   and mostly i am tired of
not healing completely but we have come so far   for so much for this life
our life growing heavy   against your peritoneum i will go further i will not
stop i cannot

Scooby-Doo [Great Dane, Crystal Cove, 1969]
after questioning Paul Muldoon

Fred only seeks out the soluble,
the same mysteries ending
I would have got away with it
were it not for you meddling all.

Not the case of the father
who turned the hunting rifle
on himself three minutes after
he destroyed his daughter.

Something must have stayed
Nerval's hand the night
he finished himself
that sailed past this father.

I would like to pull both masks
see one idea clarified in one face
and one idea clarified in the other.

What did you do at work today dad

I presented to someone
The sheer reality their dreams must scale
I did not go into detail
I did not tell them
I do not know where the loose rocks lie
That the view from the lower slopes is
Alright   once
You get used to it

Oh, I just
Sent some emails.

Square

Liam was fed up with people saying he was vanilla.
I'll show you all, he said,
And lowered his balls into a Dyson Air Blade ™
They settled in the gutter; two grapes
Making love in the skin of a chicken thigh.
Afterwards,
If anything,
The number of men
Washing their hands in that bathroom
Actually went up a bit.

Holism

I saw a chiropractor once who resembled
a poet I loved who loved an older farmer
who was married to a woman instead
instead. He had been a gymnast, a specialist
in the rings, on the national team of a Baltic state.
The chiropractor, that is. The poet
became a distiller and is sought after now
for his spirits. He lives in Ovid where
he grows the grain, a Demeter of sorts. Ovid,
New York. It was quite intimate, the session—
holistic, he called it—in which I was asked
to connect to some shame or regret or rage
as he adjusted. I was to speek freely.
I presented with some immobility,
a lessening range in my shoulder girdle, which
he explored while I lay or turned and gave over
or said I did to the emotion. I wanted to
be a good case for him. It was their lashes
and bovine eyes and overall compactness
that they shared. To the poet I admitted
my crush, invited him to my dorm room
expressly to do so. I remember we each
leaned our temples to the wood frame of
the top bunk between request and letdown.
Bodies mirror each other in empathy. I wanted him
not to feel bad not wanting me. He had
a habit, funny now, and fell into it then:
to unbutton his shirt when he spoke, especially
about poetry, the love we shared. Outside
the loblolly pines shook free some snow
and rebounded. The chiropractor stood
where my feet could press against his thighs,
held them a little, and lit a final question:
Have you, this winter, slipped and braced the fall
with your left hand, perhaps while holding,

securing, protecting something in your right?
I could not prop on my elbows so I stared
still at the ceiling, not yet reaching
for my shirt. I flashed on my slip down the stairs
and the coffee all over the landing
that had splashed despite my grip on the mug.
It had been two or three months since, and
I had sprung up, not much hurt but stunned.
It was as though he had choreographed it.
How did you know that?
Later, I'd have to stop seeing him, since
his remedies were all wrong—a protracted
process to overcome the certainty that I could
surrender more to his sureness—but I don't
deny the magic of his answer.
                              Where it hurts
is how it happened. That is always true.

Outpost

On whose behalf this dry wood scent,
sawdust in it, balsa, in the last half hour
of sun, enters, fatherly, no one
says. It is to exact a tax, too
exact a tax, or it is a benefice he
delivers the parson of the community
trust he says secures their mutuality.
The parson opens his cerebral hands and thanks
the emissary, each time a new parishioner,
an elder, never yet another bachelor,
though that is not forbidden in the alms book.
There is in that unspokenness an erotics,
as in any care not to indulge or tempt,
and the scent leaves after—not with—
the man and his embarrassed pleasantries
or deference, grudge, ambient shame, or pity.
The curate closes his month with it and presses
in his narrow palm the coins, which denominate
as kroner in rural Norway, francs in Chimay,
pence on the pound in the English midlands,
a dollar almost in Galax or Sewanee.
The vestige outside oeconomy, younger
than any of the trees I in his memory
oversee in the last finger of sun, gleaming
then shut to silhouette, like the vireo
on this post, black drop of partridge
as if stood on no leg at all. It had been there
not a moment ago, half contour like the moon,
half planar, like the chip riven by the ax,
good for a pop in the night's fire, reading
Ibsen or Eliot: Scenes of Clerical Life.

Masculinity

That man who called me a moron
as I waited for his daughter to cross the road.

The man who shouted DING DING at me
when I paused mid-cycle to let his dog have a piss.

That man who backed his car into my bike
and pointed a finger, saying

if you touch my car again I won't be so nice to you.
All of us have gone through something

that makes us suppose these responses are normal.
Trying to get to sleep

I imagine hugging each of them in turn,
telling them everything's okay.

This makes me less anxious, but I guess
they'd be furious.

The Rain Falls as Whispered Love Letters

from widows   and I almost wrote my own   spent eight hours
drafting it over the phone   each word a rancorous pill to swallow
each pause a kind chug from the noosed-neck of a bottle of wine   I
comb over the would-be-autopsy report   read the snug details of
effect with no mention of cause   it is the finished article not the
keystrokes that pined its creation   it is the finished masterpiece
coded *abandonment*   the body is like a glass   it can only hold so
much before it spills out over the bathroom floor   flooding the
kisses that will never again be pressed to your lips   I have never
hated writing something so much before   knowing that silence had
become your unwelcomed friend   and even though your rain did
not fall today   I know that one day it will pour

Fledgling

the day has drowned   you are miles away from sea
in that little port you call home

we move like birds   flocking to wherever the sun
calls   wanting to claim some warmth

beyond the messy nest we've made   that
longing for our wings to feel

more than the defeat of the sea breeze   the need of the
sun's soft caresses   those fireworks

cheering the upset of nightfall's apocalypse   where
the tides dance like drunken angels

around the harbour's hollow trumpet call   how often do you
lose yourself

beneath the current of your duvet   your pillow
the only float you can cling to

against the flaying of the waves   how often do the things
you think have washed away

return   the way the wind beats back the gull
beak unable to rip through the

stormed darkness that lurks above the vastness of
the sun's reaches   how often

do you take yourself to the window   feel the moon's
tender clutch release you

Fair

It's silly to refer to a gun as an arm
        better to call it a penis
        the way it spits forth masculine empowerment.

Can I sell you a second penis?
        I think you want one, don't you?
        This one is very good
        it's automatic
        and I can fit it with a silencer
        so no-one knows
        you're using your second penis.

Ding-dong!

Here's my suggestion:
        next time you pass an event billed as an arms fair
        go back in the dead of night
        and change all the signage to 'penis fair'
        and then go back in the morning
        and watch all the mad middle-aged menopausal men
        queueing up for their second penis.

(and then lock all the doors from the outside and burn the fucking place
down. (oh that wasn't me talking; that was the missus.))

Men

Old men listen to their lungs
creaking the springs in the bed.

Young men shoot ahead their semen.

Life is absurd, said Harry. I've got a telescope trained on a distant star. It has a fulsome lens.

Has anyone, or anything, offered any suggestion whatsoever to your fulsome lens, asked Jack.

No, said Harry, life is absurd.

Motherhood

> *That night in the field, all the eggs basketed inside me*
> *lay down with me when I lay down*
> *next to the man who would not*
> *be the father of my daughters...*
> — Cecily Parks, "Motherhood"

You came home tipsy from a girls' night out
    And read me a poem you'd found while scrolling Twitter—
        As one of your friends was going on about
            Her husband's weakness for the babysitter.

You loved this poem, though you were afraid to show it,
    And not because ten years ago you swore
        You hated reading poems, and being a poet,
            And just could not be bothered anymore,

And not because while you were with your girls,
    I was convincing ours to go to bed,
        Their teeth swiped clean, a comb run through their curls,
            Their foreheads kissed, their favorite stories read,

But, maybe, because it was a poem of love,
    And not for the man the poet was married to,
        Nor for the girls she was the mother of,
            But for the cad who'd slept with her in lieu

Of his own much-loved, much-wronged, much-offstage wife,
    A wife he'd never truly meant to leave,
        Any more than he'd meant his talk of a new life,
            Despite the young poet's longing to believe,

And maybe because this poem for a married man
    Was a surrogate for a poem you would not write,
        About a different, likewise married man,
            On a different, likewise unencumbered night,

And because, although the title of this poem
    Was "Motherhood," it mentioned terms like *mother*
        And *children* and *father* and *marriage* and *homelife* and *home*
      Scarcely at all, in favor of another

More urgent and enthralling set of words,
    Words like *yes, stranger, craving, touch,* and *youth,*
        In lines that swooned with flowers and beasts and birds
        And sounded, to your sick heart, like the truth.

Public Statement

First, I must give my thanks to everyone
Who has, over the last few weeks, made clear
The gravity of what I've said and done,
However difficult this was to hear.

Second, I offer my apologies,
Humble, sincere, wholly inadequate,
To those I've injured. On my hands and knees
I ask you to forgive, but not forget.

As of today, I formally renounce
My station, title, privileges, and fame,
And though I understand the gesture counts
For precious little, I renounce my name.

Let it be known: The man I've always been
Is finished. You won't hear from him again.

Sando

from Tagalog – [noun] sleeveless undershirt

When they speak of the Second Coming
like all kids do on a Saturday afternoon,

they say Jesus will take you first
because you have always been the nicest, you

who doesn't pick at the santan flowers,
who never bothered to impress the girls

or size up to the boys.
How amusing they found you,

their little pet,
chasing around the afternoon,

so unaware of your body
and its lack of muscle,

straps of a white undershirt clinging
onto thin, weightless shoulders.

Dr. Frankenstein Explains

All the way through school it was the same:
'Don't be such a cissy, Frankenstein,
you're a big boy now...'

And so they'd pull me, coaxing, mocking,
from the only games that gave me any pleasure.

Boys, I was told, make machines, are inventors
especially of things that fight and kill;
girls get first the dolls and then the babies
to hold and watch with love and wonder.

So they pushed me into science – you're a boy,
learn how things tick, be logical, ambitious,
no more cissy games; if you become a man
you can be anything you want...

I thought about this   I became
a great scientist   I thought about this.
I wanted to sit in a quiet corner with a child.
I wanted to feel the warmth of life continuing.

My labour has finished, or just begun.
I have, in man's way, become a mother.
Here is my child: isn't he beautiful?

That's the Question

What does the woman do?
She does the shopping, feeds the kids, cleans the house,
scrubs, dusts, hoovers, washes, cooks, irons, darns, tidies,
walks and walks and stands and walks and stands and works.

What does the man do?
He goes to work, he goes to the pub, he watches the telly.

What does the woman do?
She has a nervous breakdown and can't do anything.

What does the man do?
In this case he sits and he cries
because he can't clean, scrub, dust, hoover –
can't cook, iron, darn, tidy.

You ask, is this true?
I say yes, a friend told it to me
as I tell it to you.

You ask, is that really a man
if he can't do these things to look after himself
and another too?

Ah, that's the question, isn't it?

Protectorate

For Laura

One thing my sister never did
was slip me out at midnight
to join her at parties, where
sitting around the fire I
tremulously sipped drinks
and watched her older friends
exchange like trading cards:
glances, Wrigley's, cigarettes.
Nor when my ball had dribbled
against our juiced-up neighbour's car
one too many times did she pin him
with her heel pressed into the soft
part of his thigh nor, staring up at him,
tell him to *go ahead, make her day,*
though on the night we had to move away
she did guide me under the silver birch
and with a kitchen knife carved our names
into the peeling bark, and years later
planted that same tree, pendulous,
like its own room, and watched me,
as I walked her daughter underneath,
surveying every citizen of her state.

Which Way Round It Is

I am discovered by my daughter
on her expedition
across the cheap red rug
that won't stop moulting
so when she eats
porridge has capillaries
spaghetti lengths are blood shot.

My legs on the sofa
torso on the floor
she looks down at me
then up, concludes
this familiar, traffic-stopping lump
must have dropped from the UFO lampshade
and its glass-pear bulb-womb
according to
the same cherry blossom rules
that sometimes blears houses to the right
while her insides softly orient
like deep sea fauna
that migrate tentatively,
one sightless calamari millimetre per hour.

Just-born-useless,
dumb as chimneys mouthing nothing at aloof 747s,
I have been waiting forever
for her to arrive with her genius
to explain me to me.

Tower Hamlets Road

You have found your way home. You wait outside for too long and
everyone goes to bed. You don't have a key so you crack the old glass on
the shed door to get in and pull out a lounger to sleep on; you want to look
at the stars and try hear what they are whispering about why Betelgeuse is
at 73% of its usual brightness, and getting dimmer.

All the noise you are making wakes dogs and they start to howl. You get
briefly lit by the passing blue lights of a police car: the siren is off. You have
cut your hand and now bleed a version of Britain. You briefly remember a
friend.

The next morning your family don't suspect it had been you. They don't
think you exist anymore. Once, your youngest crayoned what he thought
happened to you. In the wood, there isn't a tree branch that doesn't offer
its bleak service. The weather repeatedly happens but there's no oomph to
it. You wonder if it is a Thursday. Possibly a Friday.

It's Monday. Again.

Eye-Test, Earls Court Square

You were leaning on the bar looking out beyond the gain line,
with a wine glass in one hand, your confidence in the other.
I was still skinny, waiting in what might have been a queue.

When you gave me the eye, a big come-hither, I smiled back,
feeling younger than I really was and so much less capable
than you have always been: your deft poems steeped in more.

Now, here we are again, in Bloomsbury, in our latest decade,
celebrating your publisher's birthday. I watch you bustle past
while some of us wait in the stalls, hoping to catch a signature.

Seamus and Ted aren't here in person and it has been so long
since I failed your eye-test, slipping away to a middle row seat.
You may have left, but here I am observing where you passed.

After Tennis

My first serve called out, correctly and often.
Your groundstrokes passing me with ease.
What was not lost on the tennis court
had typically disappeared by the time
we reached the swimming pool.
All that splash and laughter echoed
in the cluster of working barns and stores.

Later, our swimming having finished,
nearly silent water lapped and glinted.
Those beech trees somewhere down the hill
would greet us with their dappled shade,
although I hoped for more than that.
An early lesson in patience and denial
while you maintained a proper distance.

Photo of a Memory on Fire

We're three years away
      and we're taking silly photos on the train

Naivety gets the better of us as I lull my head onto your shoulder
      An intimate, unfortunate, act

The table of four behind us
      hoods up with their North Face puffers, puffing their chests out

                Masculinity doesn't get better than this

Us, wrapped in wool, linen and corduroy
      May as well have worn clown noses

An intimate act turned minute and mammoth in the same fragile exhale
      and knocks the wind out of us in the stale train carriage

A table of four,
      faceless, behind our backs

but not forgettable
      Hidden within the low quality selfie

now years within our camera rolls

Constellations Around Your Ear

Blurry Bathroom Mirror
i haven't taken a good look at you in a while, really

booze booming in my ears
        to make myself feel a little more
                me
or perhaps not quite
              so

Blurry Mirror in the bathroom, stay —
        just look at the eye bags on this face

i bought glitter eyeliner as a spur of the moment purchase
        and now i face the consequence
of attempting to put it on my blotchy face

the music is pounding outside
        it's like jazz that's missed a beat

fuck it
        i think, but don't say, as i graffiti my face with gold sparkles
that i'll find out later is far more difficult to wash off
        than i initially anticipated

              second guessing
              the morning after guilt
                  already settled in my face

quick rinse
        face cleansed for a brief cacophonous   moment
before giving another attempt

the g*y agenda
        lies in glitter and concealer

my rough skin rejecting the dainty spectacle
       as i gather the strength to un-think

Blurry Mirror
there's constellations around my ears
and I'm not quite ready

to feel

The world is an emergency but, at the Butlins '90s Weekender, everything feels hunky dory

Fuck you Dylan Thomas.
The three of us are here. In this massive auditorium,
all these forty-something men around us, bellies and pints.
Turin Brakes are singing save me. Save me from myself.
Words from my easy days. All leisure and nonchalance and
I'm trying my best to be present in our collective pasts.
Old friends, out west, together, some post-shoot out, cowboy's lucky finish.
None of us have told our kids how we've had to survive to get this far.
We've pretended we were raised in long, hop-field summers.
Green and carefree, like you taught us.
We've also told them their world will be pretty much the same
as ours has been, something they already know is a lie.
Someone burnt the Old Barn to the ground to get the insurance
and we're laughing about that. Up on stage, they've started singing
Don't leave me here on my own. Those same sad chords. This different time.
Singing it over and over.

Fuck you Dylan Thomas.
That's no way to deal with fear. Besides,
what did you actually know about chains and dying.
However much you revealed in the idea of destruction,
the Soviets had no real claim on your estuarine landscapes,
your skylarks and hillsides. Perhaps you'd prefer it now?
I'll bet that swallow thronged loft of yours is blighted by wings
no more, and it might interest you how glorifying
the stewardship of fields has turned out all ill judged and wrong.
The existential horror is within the system.
But what do I know? People like me are just here to work,
Monday to Friday, to kick back in consumption at the weekends
and there are cheap burgers at the bar. Undefined meats.
Rows of sauces. Barbecue. Sweet mustard mayonnaise.
There are all these men tapping their feet as they drink themselves to death.

All those poets pushing phrases around a page too. This burning world
an incidental backdrop. Our children carrying the can.
Carrying it over and over.

Quick Ornithological Quiz

And so yesterday's right answer was cock
        not inclined to colourful clothing
                and cock's choice of a mid-range feather
and cocks finding contentment or full of guilt
        alone above the brimming water

and cocks that are liable to act out like tigers
        cocks preferring to live modestly enough
                while cocks express a preference for patterns
rich yet broad as their clamorous wings
        and perhaps any particular cock on occasion

enjoys isolation yet today's right answer
        is that cocks tend to favour fruit
                (but they are not averse to tackling meat)
that cocks cover great distances at twilight
        (but will always find their own way home)

that cocks like to hang with clever people
        (by implication people like themselves)
                though it's true cocks can be rather common
they are enormously resourceful
        to be honest cocks have such busy minds

(which is why some can be indecisive
        torn between passion and/or commitment
                no better than crows on black dog days)
and morph then into proper loners
        though if given a tree of a decent height

and once impressed by a reasonable cause
        and if left for a few quiet hours together
                a cock can recover an outburst of song
quite un-cock-like though this year's answer
        is that cocks are keeping their heads down

anticipating storms so your journal entry
        (hoping this year's brood stand tall in the air
                before heaven turns grey before them)
is wrong—too many companionable wings
        have gone missing—

Nebamun hunting

18th Egyptian Dynasty

Astride a flimsy raft of otherworldly reeds
in profile—no time for perspective—

his daughter set at last in her proper place
small and between his legs

one hand clinging tenderly to his left shin
similarly his barely responsive wife

is transfixed now letting him finish—
great Nebamun—accountant to the pharaohs

finds there is deserving and purchase of place
to hunt through the wild marshes

of the ineluctable afterlife
where the oversized shape of a marmalade cat

is really a sun god greedily taking down
three birds at once and all the fishes

shoaling in the waters and all the butterflies
that animate the air are the forces

of chaos that he can now waft away
with the fear of balances that will not tally

Across Clapham Common

And I walk alone
in a city wept of its men
and what we do.

Last week, in early Spring,
I'd cock my head, maybe smile.
But here, a Crocus. I'll retreat.

Mixology of My Maleness

Coming up in my baggy self. Shine
that fatherlight onto me. Overlapping
spot-circles. Born. Cartoon villain Dick
Dastardly. I'll deftly deify
whatever in that vein. Goofing
with mates and buddies is a dry
ice sort of understanding. Forgive me
one TikTok rendition of the sickling
son. Making tricksy shots from someone's poorly-
fitting pedestal. Call me Crazy Beard, waxing
quite eloquent. I am darling, downplayed.
Playing dom and acting doofus.
Say, there goes that bloke, ungainly
and un-dangerous. So seldom set upon.
Scantily sexy, it's unsaid. They deem me
brazen as the palest fire.

In Fantasies of Retribution, I am Just

Here in a toy shop. I grow scared
at the child's *raar!* and *peew!*
Momentarily. His white eyes
are painted on. Aromas
of Plasticine. And, faintly,
train set moss. He manhandles
two WWF figurines.
Their names might be
Flopcrusher or Wimpwrangle.
Both heroes forcibly clashed.
Mano a mano. Wrestled
toward a zero sum. The upshot:
stranglemate. Faintly,
I can locate Airfix cement.
A scent of Lego manuals.
The way one larger boy
once pressed my legs
into my chest. The way
bricks suffer blows
and bounce. I need to breathe,
I informed him. Fairness
forced to the intestines.
Evacuating the play scene.

The Last Time

No one knows the last time is happening
as the last time happens. For example,
today is my ex-best friend's birthday
and I think about him more in five minutes
than I imagine he's thought about me
in as many years. I still see his wild eyes
in every bottle of Captain Morgan
and whenever I hear my favourite
band's biggest riff – or his. He used
to pick me up and we'd sing
and bitch hard in supermarket car parks
deep into the morning hours,
even with brightening skies
warning us of our looming shifts.
I'd Snapchat his rants and we'd ignite
belly laughs that burnt so long
they nearly made us sick. But
I can't tell you the last time
we did any of this. And I feel
as if he's just made me laugh again
after tearing out my heartstrings.

i've been to therapy

three times. three times
i've been to therapy.
i feel it's important
to start with that fact.
because a male YouTuber
is making fun of therapy
in front of a million eyes
right now. he has an issue
with people who say
they're in therapy
on the front cover
of their dating profile
(and he also believes
no men bake!). it reminds me
of my team's star striker -
a man who stands
at six and a quarter foot
with a body built
like a Roman column -
when he laughed on a podcast
at men who cry. *pathetic,*
he said. *get a grip!*
don't get me wrong,
i still wildly cheer
his goals with men
who think romantic comedies
are guilty pleasures
because in my teens,
i thought poor mental health
was a weakness.
and with that confession
out in the open,
should any man
want to whisper

or shout
their darkest thoughts
out loud,
my ear will always
be here.

Apprenticeship

for decades
  i have knelt

onstage
  pressing

my lips
  to the damp

wood
  over which

a trumpeter
  in smoke &

darkness
  swings

his green
  silk notes

who are you?
  i whisper

how long
  will this last?

he never
  answers

without
  looking down

he drains
  his spit valve

into my open
  mouth

Diary Entry: February 16, 1994

The central focus of life should not be flesh.
Masculinity is not defined by
muscularity, beard growth, and testicle size.

I've learned I can't force my body to change—
but I can control behavior.
I tell myself: If you want to be a man, act like one.

Principled Uncertainty

End stage:
In this epoch, at this age,
        baggage too becomes relative,
Everyone speaking
        about "chosen" careers
Like they're advocating
        for remaining dry
during *that* thought experiment
        with the lifeboat
        and insufficient supplies,
Forcefully
        giving reasonings for *why*,
as the climate appears hostile,
        as does the sky,

History never repeats itself, but it does often rhyme.

And some histories,
        decontextualized over time,
Are flaws wounding fatally,
Are a drawstring bag of all the winds,
daring you to set them free...

A Fixed Point for Navigation

In the breathless lacuna: We were always moving,
even in our stillness. And space is littered
with frozen bodies, the vacant husks
of long, lost time travellers who neglect this,
who forget the expansion of the universe,
mirrored in the expansion, of the heart, of a mind, constant
and accelerating dilations, progressing exponentially,
expressing non-linear change, conditional on decay.

Nothing outside a substance can cause it to exist.
And everything must have a cause.
So, a substance must cause itself to exist.

Ours is perpetually possibilities exploding into being,
and time is breathless stillness, even as it flies
and you ask me what I am thinking,
and instantly, my head empties of all meaningful discourse,
usurped by the arriving husks, the frozen bodies
of my infinite future selves trying to revisit this version of us.

Shopping With Michael

She likes Santini tomatoes but he says they're shitey little yokes so she pops the bigger ones into the trolley. She'll get herself a pack during the week, when he's up at his mam's.

His socks won't be dry in time for the gun club meeting so she turns on the radiators, just for an hour. To be sure.

The duvet covers in the bargain basket in Dunnes look nice but he says he doesn't like the colour mauve and anyway they have the big buttons and annoy his toes.

The woman on the checkout chats tittle tattle and who's joined the unending list on rip.ie, he frowns and rattles the trolley's child seat before handing her the cash.

She mentions a fundraiser, the mental health thing up in the club. He says not-at-all, why would you be giving money when there's new balls needed for the under twelves.

She'll take the a few bob out if his pocket when he's asleep and drop it in during the week, please god. Later, he catches her going through his pockets.

Why?

Because you dismantled me
with pedagogic knuckles

and

the slip of priestly tongues.

The Father of Milk

Is non-toxic masculinity a paradox or a cliché you ask?
Both. Paradoxical Sterne contrived such in Toby Shandy,
the soldier who literally wouldn't hurt a fly. A soldier's son,

Sterne was born in Tipperary like my father: a marksman
in a neutral country's army who never fired a shot in anger.
Discharged himself, he'd find no work at home, so left

to serve forty years in an English dairy. I'd call him up
in that phrase out of D.H. Lawrence: "the father of milk":
kind as Toby – and just as faithful in performing his duties.

When I let my guinea pig graze on our flag-sized lawn,
he watched, an airgun in his lap to keep cats off. Young,
he had a pet hare I now imagine suckling, not from cows,

like a witch hare, but his cartoning machine. This page
is also his milk carton: I stir in 'lusna' magic spider threads
of words with the 'lámh marbh' – but I lack white magic,

my 'dead hand' is cliché and sentimentality, my milk is still
spilled, my father is still in neutral Death's army, I call up
only his ghost. I have no words. The cat got my tongue.

Portrait of the Artist as a Young Offender

In prison, Tom lifted poems
from In Memoriam columns,
flogging them to fellow cons
for letters to their loved ones

to show their personal growth,
the softer side they'd develop,
the greater sense of self-worth,
by joining a poetry workshop –

till Tom noticed, to his horror,
the poems in the papers recur,
changed only in their names . . .
If supply gave him problems,

demand had grown rampant
with his customers not men
it was healthy to disappoint.
He thought. He lifted his pen.

Sudden Departure, No Forwarding Address

Twin prop to Edinburgh
passes over the Copelands
cruising toward land
with a constant hum

At this altitude, cumulus
are snow-covered hills
opening to silver lakes
and endless possibilities

The plane tilts, turns,
pockets of turbulence
ghost light on the propeller
as I merge with the clouds

What to jettison from this life
of many starting overs
with the imaginary god
of second chances.

ON TENDERNESS
by Luke Nilan

It's starting to sound natural when I say to myself
I got to go feed the birdies.
The birdies.
I saw these growing signs of tenderness
in my own aging father,
and now I'm catching the condition.
Those last years, he would take me by the shoulders,
smile, say 'Lukie my son!'
His eyes teary when I'd say goodbye.

They says this happens
when the testosterone slips away.

Don't get me wrong,
I was often a pretty sweet guy
when I wasn't being an SOB.

The birdies are all set for the day.

Luke Nilan: a fictional 75-year-
old poet, from an unpublished
manuscript

I want my people to be okay

after a FraternityX clip where a bottom kicks a top in the face after saying "stop" three times, ignored

, to need not kick against oppressors,
to not discern nor view those around
us un-gawked. I want my people content
with the crook of an arm, safe holiday
defining not what else dark remains
a shard in our ruined sight – to feel
fine, I guess, sitting out the toxic
consideration. I don't want the gutted
image, a repeating clip, a mass-shooting,
the gang scene. I want my people to not
fall even under desperate terms about
my people, meekly screamed. To need not
pray. To aerate hotel rooms with prayers
anyway. I want strong men to look then
cry, to feel not foot on jaw nor fetish
nor vanilla judgement, the studio empty
with healing, forgiveness furious to witness
our gross undertaking. For this my people
may say we should sing our thank yous
when the ends dry out, clothes performed
without truthful stinking matter, no
pathetic spittle at hand for my people
to be soaked, spreading, a startled stamen
in the cracked flowerhead, a laughing man
who does not do what necessary evil
curtails all seeking men to lose because
, my people, I need a prayer, okay,
for already it is too late. I see nothing

ahead of me but hope, perishing.

A fear extinguished in the rain.

The human heart, capitulating.

Boss : Liquid Snake (Top of Metal Gear REX)
After Metal Gear Solid by Hideo Kojima & Tomokazu Fukushima

Now you know.

I was birthed

with one purpose:

to be the petri dish

run-off, the surplus

test tube scrapings,

nothing but

primordial sludge

bound for a canary-

coloured bin.

Just recessive

alleles injected

in an unwitting egg,

forced to watch

a twin take

flesh – a lab-grown

doppelganger,

leeching

all my purest

chromosomes.

You. My brother.

Every masterpiece

has its charcoal

sketched first draft

& I was yours. Our

Government guinea-

pigged me

so they could craft

you: a soldier

with prime

killer instinct coded

in his genome.

We, both of us,

were factory-line

facsimiles of

our father:

Big Boss, the world

famous fighter.

There were others

too. Don't you

mourn our siblings –

those fruitless ova,

the sluggish sperm

cells we slaughtered

to survive? Yes, all

men are murderers

before the day

they're born.

The real reason

you came here this

chill Alaskan night

is no green beret

call of duty;

a butcher's bloodlust

lurks within

your genes.

danny zuko turned jock
After Grease *(Dir: Randal Kleiser)*

pearlies cream as his purewool rydell sweater // he discoes through the parched carny grass // crimps his cuffs // cool as the term-end breeze: *that's right, i did* // quiff-tips droop // but he stays grease slick // glides to the side // of the one he's always wanted // a cadillac soars // on a bluescreen sky //

Pineapple Rings and Dostoyevsky

the young, wannabe writer,
pale, a deep sleeper,
with a morbid fear of being
thought dead as he dozes,
writes a precocious note
for a bedside table saying
should you find me like this don't
bury me for five days, better safe

than sorry. This comes back
on the day of his fake execution.
waiting his turn with a firing-squad,
facing a pre-dug grave,
he swears if there's a way to gain
a day – a red sun, this mist afloat
over pinking, Petersburg cobbles,
he will write, *'the sunlight was lovely.'*

Two men walk away from the chippy,
and weather and sport, the latest slew
of political travesty,
won't do for chatter today.
Evasion, banter, bluster,
can't disguise the anguish
in the shaking trees, walking
the winding path home.

One man stops, says to the trees,
'It's my heart, mate.' Some men
bare their nipples to the moon
at such news, grease their face, howl,
and if straight-nosed Romans on passing
titter at their simple costume and gaudy
woad, so what? But 'you done with them?'

is all the other says, one eyebrow raised
to the crying man's pineapple rings
in batter, sticky and salty and sweet.

The Laughter of Mustard and Sea Foam

We're not bedside vigil
or drawn ward curtains,
forced banter or hushed
voices on a waterbed

of solace. We won't
discuss the death
of elephants as a proxy
for the loss

of our neurodivergent
from societal shaming.
We're not backslapper
blokey, we don't reek

bonhomie. We grind
words like pebbles, rolled
round the mouth, and taste
the grit in our saliva.

You went to save a party
at the late-night store,
but didn't read a label
properly and haul home

32 cans of 0% alcohol.
You hate to be laughed at.
You spun a girl around
the red wine room on huge

grey shoulders for the whole
of Heaven 17's 'Temptation',
4 minutes 37 seconds in
the 12-inch version.

We followed a Mobius strip
of double yellows through
the city till we found the end
of the thread down our local.

I grab this moment to say
your yellow coat for safari
may upset the elephants,
who mistake you for a banana.

'I's not yellow', you say,
'I's mustard and seafoam.'
Which cracks us up.

The Flight

Let's just say it's Sunday already
and go to the church, full of silk
and wine spilling from broken cups,
tears leaking from eucharistic
connections, as if we really were free
once and for all. Silly jokes and sly
capitulation to the lack of a remedy.
It's not as if any of this is a mystical secret.

Sir, I keep my mouth shut completely
unless some daemon up and prompt
me into accident and embarrassment, outbursts
of Sibylline music. Orlando di Lasso!
You have shown us the route
and the method and we give our assent.
Stand up straight and walk away,
in a straight line, immune to gravity.

Orlando di Lasso (1532-94), polyphonic composer, was repeatedly abducted as a child because of the beauty of his singing.

Salmacis / *Hermaphroditus*

She knew this time something was wrong.

> *He knew for a long time something was wrong.*

She scanned the midwife's silence: it ran full-term.

> *He scanned his body each morning, heard her heart racing.*

She needed twenty-four hours to reach a decision.

> *He needed twenty-four years to reach a decision.*

She would bear her daughter's parts for spare.

> *He could bear to spare his mother's feelings no more.*

She chose to save one child with another.

> *He chose to be them/they/their.*

Lost Property

Yes, I have baggage—you gif
with camp counterpoint to the serious
seam we seem to be threading; I ping
back an emoticon that can't decide
if it's laughing or crying—*don't we all, Hun.*

Until now, we've offered ourselves only
fetish-fleshed and, seductively shiny,
have rebuffed all scrutiny. I feel flattered
you feel able to unzip a little, reveal
the wound we all gaily carry.

Pink and perfumed as an orifice,
I'm disgusted/delighted as you proceed
to pull soiled smalls from it: Ta-Dah!
Trauma! Disorder! Dependence
on drug-divined euphoria!

My own fissure has been long-sutured
by a miscellany of therapies, weeps only
modestly/manfully; yours is still seeping
through a recent addressing.
I nightingale a hard-won song—

some like to dance around hand-luggage,
I prefer to unpack it. You smile,
in simulacrum; our thread darts
through gym routines and other less
weighty material then, on the hem

of our next hookup, is abruptly cut.
Receiving no reciprocation—not even
a tick of acknowledgement—I apprehend
a deep thrum, the transmission
of pain, as though you are in me again

and circling the case you left, closed
in my head, I trace an arc between
markers of the places you've been,
from abandonment to rehabilitation,
mourn my misplaced projection

in which you allow yourself to be
unlocked—soft-furnishings
spilling/spreading; lungs for lampshades,
guts for garlands—and make of me
your home.

Select all images with fire hydrants

The pedestrian crossing.
The yellow school bus.
The abandoned bicycle.
The anxious traffic lights
saying click me, click me,
bring some life back
to these desiccated pixels
where it's a crime scene
waiting for jumpy snipers.
Skip when you no longer
see assault rifles, blades,
syringes or burnt crosses.
You will qualify as human
unless you fail 200 times
when dark suited agents
will emerge to escort you
to secure meta-facilities.
Close family members
will be alerted in person.
They will say your son
is not who you thought.
Your uterus carried a case
of mistaken identity
smart enough to pass
as a man with viable skin
and plausible relationships
until we caught him out
when he failed to identify
a taxi/bridge/chimney.
Not your legal fault.
You may now kiss him
goodbye if you can click
every square on the grid
that contains love until
no more remains.

Glass Courage

The window of my son's taxi rises.
Back in the flat, his fingerprints
confect the mirrors with whorls.
A hurricane has hit the bathroom.
There will be socks and underpants,
coat hangers leaving question marks
everywhere because he is my son.
An ID document will be forgotten.
A teapot will be hidden in tea towels
cooling the amber warmth inside.
I would never have shouted back
'I love you' with his lion
in my voice had he not roared it first.

Two Ships

Open the door to your brother
shrinking on the top-step.

A bottle of cider under his arm
phone cracked on the grass.

You could ask him what happened
but you already know the answer.

It's in the lines on his face
the clouds in his eyes.

The way he turns his wedding ring
as if to stop would burn his skin.

And rain as heavy as the Atlantic
would burst forth to drown him.

Stand aside, push back the door
feel his gait brushing yours.

Place your hand on his shoulder
give him room to enter.

August

My unhappiness at the present is that I am jealous of the past.
— Soren Kierkegaard

When my friend's wife travels for work he regresses
to a time when all he had was a cash in hand job
and a law class we were too hungover to attend.
Mid-days we smoked and rehashed the same old lines,
the hue of our home towns the plan for the future
to be useful was blasphemy for the day was long
and in a second gone so we'd better not leave the house.

Infinity has no direction yet he tries to reverse it anyhow,
calls in sick, stocks up on snacks, drives to an overpass,
picks-up. On a kitchen top, grinds and rolls and binds
with a roach, to the window to veil the sun falls
on the couch lights-up, life elongates but in a good way.
Fleeing the fundamentals he stays like this for weeks,
trips to the bathroom a sudden sharp shift when she calls.

He lie's and lies from silent fog to mental cold from tourist
to participant we must change the day before it's late.
Sunday my friend's wife returns. Monday he replies.
Apologises for the distance: *It all flew-by in an instant*
and now he has to work in an environment where minutes
move in increments. We rearrange to meet but we put it off.
September, my turn to wade in the mire like clockwork.

Jung Snr in the After

You are dead, father;   you have no coordinates.
You're now nowhere   and nowhen. I feel you
Stood at the edge of   the circle, eaves

                                                          dropping,

You desire the latest   information
you now realise you   should have sought
     when you had/   were in time. You seem cross.

There have been   related

several cameos   in the dreams of close relatives in which
you intimated   and beckoned well enough, floating, semi-
t   r   a   n   s   p   a   r   e   n   t   ,
and were only once   recalled on waking,

if not fully

                                                  understood.

I theorise from here: you are *primordial image,*
   a diffuse cloud of   *cognition surrounding*
what no longer has   *ordinates and abscissae.*[1]

---

1. **Urbild,** eine diffuse Wahrnehmungswolke umgibt ohne ordinaten und

abszissen...

Prince Five Weapons Leaves School

What "Once upon a time in a land far away" really means is "Now and always happening everywhere, including here."
— Rubem Alves

I am a pregnant man now.
I carry an unborn thunderbolt
Of the kind a prince might grow.
Confidently into the forest

I strut into the realm
Of the ogre Stickyhair.
Armed, with my full womb.
Ready, steady, aware.

My weapons all stick fast
To the unharmed beast.
I knew they would. I do not fret.
A power burns in my belly.

Like a lion of a man,
Tamed at the right time,
Fed on the light.
Hear the rumble of me

Come down from the mountain.
Ego cibum fructum/the fruit ate me.
Inside I nurture a fountain, which
I pour forth from my mouth over the ogre.

The beast is conquered.
All ears and no teeth.
Now, he receives my scion s/word.
I pierce him with my sixth.

a charm against domestic violence

I said
I can't speak of
the violence that
went unseen

you're safe
as none of us needs
go unseen   let me
say what can't be

am I?
for those who know
how it feels
to hear the latch

(click)   *(click)*
and feel glad
and feel alone
and feel afraid

am I safe?
when I was touched
a reflex flickered
will I be attacked?

what am I?
I didn't say no
didn't leave
didn't fight back

what am I?
I didn't speak
when soft fingers
crushed a fist

what are they?
when the violent
are blind to their
own violence

they are
feeling each rage
as another incident
in their suffering

I'm saying
the hurt in a fist
is less than not
being believed

are you safe?
if what had happened
hadn't? if what hadn't

happened had?
I said
what really happened?
when I can describe
each time
              she said
she couldn't remember
when she hit me   but
she remembers one time
             what are you saying?
that I can't remember
she says she's sure
there was a reason
she says
she wasn't like this
before what she
endured as a child
           I said
fists and their acts
are gestures
for her to own
I'm saying
what I can forgive
is given in what
I'm saying
          we're safe
I know in time
we will heal
given time
saying
we'll be safe
we will?
we will heal
          will we?
we will
when we dwell
in empathy
I'm saying
we will
when we dwell
in the imagination
          saying
we're safe
when the saying
has a home

Poem

She takes a glass of water to bed
On his birthday
A gold projection on his face
She reveals treasure
Beneath the wrap of her trench coat

She takes a glass of water to bed
On holiday
Shimmering ink drops
Sit upon her torso
He is a desperate man reaching
Gazing at a mirage

She takes a glass of water to bed
On a break
His in-car dialogue goes unsaid
A daytime radio play
Not broadcast
Bad choices fill the empty nights

She takes a glass of water to bed
On a reconciliation
The return of the lovers in the grass
In their matching boots
But he cannot let go
Of things best left behind

She takes a glass of water to bed
On a less frequent day
When they meet
In hotel rooms and back at her place
He slips out again
And she swears to give up this time

She takes a glass of water to bed
On a colourless dawn when he wonders
How years of your life with someone
Can only exist in a single anecdote
She has children now
And lives with her husband down south

Recreation

Between normal service and resuming
I make another journey to the town of yearning
I have taken the slow train in
Been led here by my mother's hand
And ridden the late night road out
Moments of epiphany in the backseat of a taxi ride home

This time I make Burnley stand still
The warring couple in the supermarket car park freeze mid feud
I set off to map out the exact places where Lancashire lips have met mine
The best days when you and all your friends are single
And eternal twenty-one

I know the changing face of Market Square
Because I never flattened out my accent to get on in life
I want to take a photograph
I try to get the fountain in
And the inflatable Father Christmas on top of the Co-Op
But argue with myself over composition
I take a travelator up to the balcony
And read out a love letter to the world

A nagging feeling drags me past the corner
Where The Red Lion is always reopening
Outside the Keirby Hotel I hand Harold Wilson a letter
Calling upon the USA to stop bombing North Vietnam
I rush back to stand under the clock at the bus station
And wait for my Saturday shopgirl to arrive

Across the road our Parthenon is restored
And the three daughters of Zeus play in concrete
Under a sign saying RECREATION
When my mail-order apparition doesn't arrive
I sit in a chair in a department store window
And wonder will my last thought be
Panama Joe's on a Friday night

Fault

When I am angry, and angry toward you
I am not angry *with* you
This distinction is imperative.

When foul moods find me, and they do soften
This is not your fault
Even when I make you feel that it is.

When I say I don't care, I don't mean I don't care about you
I mean I don't care about me
And you are the misfortunate mirror.

When the sun droops and fades, and the rain splat-splat-splats
It is not your fault
That I have forgotten my raincoat.

When darkness comes and I
Struggle to find my way
It is not you who has hidden it.

None of it has been your fault
But I have often made it your problem
And all of this is to say that
I do love you
Which I don't say as often as you deserve
But which I do really feel
With every day that comes.

I'm Fine

'I'm fine,' says the man to his son, but he lies.
There's always pain, it's just something he has to hide.

'I'm fine,' says the boy to the one who hurt him worst.
Not a chance he'll reveal all the tears he's cried for her.

'I'm fine,' says the guy who is nearly always drinking.
The alcohol is fatal to the thoughts that he's been thinking.

'I'm fine,' lies the man on his last and final day.
Nobody seems to notice all of the unspeakable pain.

'I'm fine,' smiles the brother, with a black suit upon his back.
Far from fine in truth, but he's not supposed to talk about that.

Their kind of man
for Dr. Denis Mukwege

He'd planned to work with kids, but then got hooked
on gynaecology, how women fought
the myths, the violence. He joined their ranks,
agreed to give a speech at the UN;
withdrew, when he got death threats to his kids.
Then he was told he couldn't go back home.

A line's been crossed. The women want him back.
They organise. They tell the government,
the men who work for them, the other men
he's under their protection. They will guard
this man around the clock, because they need
— their daughters need — him free to do his work.
The power of the women was his fuel,
he used to say. Now they've become his shield.

Breaking and entering

Not daring to hope for love,
or an invitation that might never come,
he steals what he needs from his lover;
wanting, and resenting, her
in equal measure.

Blinded to his own inner Eden,
he looks longingly at her garden,
wrongly thinking that she hides
the key to his release,
and hates her for holding it;
not seeing it has been
in his own hands
all along.

Delilah

Is it from the desire to exorcise
a deep-felt fear of softness,
and soothe the pain of our disconnection,
that we men lose what we love most;
when envy and pain distorts our delight
into rage and disdain for the beauty and grace
we crave to contain.

We sing out from stadium stands
to commemorate the love-crazed killing
of Tom's temptress from Treforest.*
But in the false safety of our sad isolation,
are we trying, and dying, to forget
our dependence on the women who reared us?

We always hurt the ones we love,
and would sooner, it seems, risk killing our Earth Mother
to extract what we think she owes us,
than live with the understanding that we are all her children,
and the knowledge that if she dies,
so do we.

1968 Tom Jones hit "Delilah", which describes the killing of his former lover by a jealous man, became an unofficial anthem for the fans of Wales' rugby team and until recently was regularly sung by them at matches. In has since been 'banned'. Tom was born and raised in the Welsh Valleys former mining town of Treforest.

Full Face

Man transfixed by a woman
doing her makeup on the tube.
His gaze a searchlight pointed
at every brush stroke.

Watches her build that picture
of pigment from goldmine
at first empty now full
of herself a construct

of pride. He wants
not for her flesh
but for the love
to do this himself.

JOE

Bagdadból érkezett a Ráday utcába,
hogy a szabadságát piával,
fiúkkal, párnák közt töltse el.
Kora tavaszi este volt, még hideg,
amikor megismerkedtünk a neten,
és egy-két szóból tudtuk a szerepet,
mert a testénél én sem akartam többet,
maradjunk meg név nélküli idegennek,
de azért koccintottuk, beszélgettünk is,
kiváncsian faggatam a munkájáról:
gyűlölte az arabokat, az embereket,
dühvel mondta, szinte vicsorogva,
és kerülte a tekintetemet.
Joe már sok embert ölhetett.
Levetkőzött. Teste, mint egy modellé,
büszke izmain tetoválások feszültek,
kemény volt és férfias, igazi katona.
Bekapcsolta a tévét, és pornót tett be,
amikor az ágyba dőlt, elnyújtózott,
nem szólt hozzám, rám se nézett,
a képernyőre meredve simogatta magát,
és várta, hogy kiszolgáljam. Kinevettem.

JOE

He was on Ráday utca from Baghdad,
hoping to spend his leave laid up
drunk in bed, with boys.
It was early Spring, still cold
when we arranged online to hook up
at the room, each knowing
our roles in a word or two, how
I only needed his body
and for us to stay nameless strangers,
but as we touched glasses and talked
I quickly asked about what he did:
he hated Arabs same as he hated anyone
came his irritated snarl,
avoiding my gaze.
He might have killed plenty.
Stripping down, he had the body
of an underwear model, tattoos
proud across all the taut muscle,
manly and hard – a real soldier.
He put porn on the TV, silently
stretching out across the bed, still
not looking at me, staring
at the screen and touching himself,
waiting to be serviced. I laughed.

Chalk Alps

Climbing, we were unsure children again
That night the ball lightning came
Over those ragged, white molars, the chalk alps,
Or, rather, incisors of some deranged, divine mouth,
Hungry for us.
In our way, I suppose, we knew. After the sun, the agony.
This mouth – or some other – would eat us. Loves transformed
To peat, as your father long had been, and mine, we knew,
Soon would be.

Hairy hands, calloused, brown, grasped ours,
Unsteady in some endless summer some thirty-years
Past, ascending and descending the hill to school.
No thought of futures, then – bright or broken – or at all.
Across the still darkening peaks and lakes
Thin, chill air. After the dope and lager,
I thought of Marie and the *Starnbergersee*,
While you slept with a smile – as she had done –
As you always have done.
At daybreak, I squatted and strained over a pit:
Daybreak in the heavens must start like this.

Dada

a baby sees me in a mask
smiles and reaches out its hand
plump with unwavering trust
says *Dada* — certain as anything —
which lights a candle in me

it doesn't matter that the babe has already learned to see their father
as black in a sea of white
that the mother avoids my face
pretends it's not happening
as her child keeps calling for who they believe me to be

all that belongs on another page
for now it's enough to notice how it felt
that I could be dada to someone
un-ridiculous
feasible

phantom

Can a thing be phantom
if it never lived or only did
in the body's mind

Does a shadow have
breadth length and depth
spreading in all three of god's directions

taking up space between
the legs   resting on thigh as though
a wish could be made flesh

A silhouette is the air'ed body of a real thing
a shape cast in dark light from something substantial
yet here we are throwing

a net of hope into the void
to catch realness
to borrow weight

It's there until it doesn't
or until you look
until you use your eyes to feel

which is another expression
for what faith is not

The boy who nobody bought flowers for

1.
When I told my ex-girlfriend nobody had ever bought me flowers
she called me a faggot
and laughed.
I've never been the best judge of character,
or good at dropping hints.
I told her that if I died
Flowers would rise from my chest and out of my throat,
and my name would change from Violet, to Lily, to Rose.
And I would have more flowers than I could hold.
But I shouldn't need to die for such abundance.
Remember, you can ask for it

2.
When I was a child, my mother bought me guns and swords.
A subtext for how the world wanted to see me,
though I will admit, I did like explosions.
But I still needed someone to pick me up when I fell,
or turn the light on when I was afraid.
And nobody gave me flowers then either,
just more swords.

Stepping in front of a bus on your lunch break

You look the same age as my son, the driver says.
His watery eyes, soften me. Now I feel bad.
We all do silly things he says, but please be careful, I don't know what I
          would've done.
He's calmer now, his shaking has stopped, he's not screaming anymore,
          which I appreciate.

The guy in the New Balance trainers insists on calling an ambulance,
even though I've assured him I'm fine, he still won't let me up.
Placing two fingers on my shoulder in a way that a big brother would.
He can fuck off.

The impact felt just like the time I got flattened at five-a-side by Gabby
          Agbonlahor's brother.
Like I was there to be hit, dutiful, on purpose.
But just like that Sunday in '07 the pain has already passed,
Out of the knees and through the mouth, only the beleaguered sensation of
contact. I'm not even quaking, but there's no guarantee how long that will
          last for.

A decision to flee is made.
Run, head down, mumble apologies and ensure nobody is in pursuit.
What to do now? Call home? Commit yourself? Take the rest of the day off?
Smoke a cigarette and go back, normal.

At the office, a colleague asks a question about Instagram.
I think. I can only hear ringing.
Sorry, what was that again? I'm real spacey today.
No worries she says, it's one of those days.

I contemplate telling her what's just happened,
blurting it out and dealing with the aftermath.
But this definitely falls under the category of NSFW,
and a trip to HR is not what I need right now.

Bando Blues

I am irresponsible, helpless & selfish. Meet a man
      named Muhammed
           on the stoop of ruin.

      He tells me,

Depression is the neighbor of loneliness,
      & you sold out the block
          like a sucker.

              I clear my throat:

     empty lots beam with fruiting bodies & dew.

          O what I've served,
            gutted—

scrapped these homes of their copper,
      my temple of its plasma, the heat
          of transmutation.

              Community lit up, bodied
                with my product.

    Remember now, love
        is like eating a strawberry.

In another state, angel dust is known as embalming fluid.

     He swallows the infinitesimal seeds:
          Ain't nothing hard about a strawberry.

Meditation on Waves in the Shape of My Father

He loved shipwrecks & he became one, his brain so delicate,
      aneurysm bursting through like steam. How water, ice, ruptures

steel as if tissue paper. I never assumed the symbolism would be
      prophecy: his split & splintering from my mother like a rift

in the hull; a sunken housing market, drowning debt; life insurance
      cashed, a raft under wavering stars. I'm swept by swelling crests

that scoop & scatter what remains of us: our unfinished basement;
      styrofoam cups of gas station coffee, cold & black;

the moccasins waiting for warmth in his blind. Lakeside memories
      surface to reflect a man within the man. I want to be alone but can't

avoid myself—make contact with every breath. *How am I even breathing?*
      I've heard the ebb will clear this wreckage, & floods will pull

us ashore to green sands. Where children sculpt the specks of this disaster
      into a castle. But hope can't dam the grieving: we've been swallowed

by an even greater hunger. It never spoke a word. Emptiness is vast,
      the ocean pales—still we tread as whitecaps carry on.

In a Country with No Sky Everyone Takes Turns to Tell Your Story

You ever hear the one about the guy who walks out of a bar & just keeps on walking? They used to tell it in good riddance country. Always talking about a guy who survived suicide attempts until he didn't. Who planned on burning bridges he jumped from to be certain there was no way back. They said that he said that it was to get rid of the need for conflict in his blood. Said he refused to fall for the con of mortality. That living forever was only possible by letting yourself die on your own terms. The way the joke goes they leave it open ended in the telling. Still, I often wonder what happened to him. I mean I know he died but I only have his word for that. There's compassion in not being completely honest if all you have is distance. You ever wonder if you get bored of living forever? I was seeing this guy once whose job it is to know things rather than believe in them. He didn't believe in much, least of all me. But had a lot of real interesting things to say about my friend. The one they talk about in stories. The one making punchlines of mythology. The guy I was seeing, who was supposed to know things & didn't believe in much, said the guy with no guts was a coping mechanism. Said he knew an author proxy when he saw one. Said it was a deficit in my ability to discern between real & imagined, but also said it was interesting I thought of myself as the surgeon rather than hero of my story. I told him that sure was a lot of words for not being able to fix me & walked off; a crowd of excuses limping, a scurry of clouds late for sky class, a boy believing least in a drowned church until he sunk which, as anyone can tell you, is when you should most believe. Stop me if you've heard this one before. This is the part where you say your name to fill in the blanks & make this history yours.

Knife Salesman

Everybody and their rustbelt wives in their scarecrow homes have knives, so the hard sell is to those more in love with the damage. Forgoing the forced charisma of desperate infomercials - the salesman's knives are better than others and he's been cutting off digits to prove it. Sure, this means he will barely make it down a street of homes before he's unable to pitch so effectively. His supplier - a few rungs up and already selling the myth of selling to the impressionable afflicted - is furious. Yes, those with knife history have bought more. But they already have knives. Once the salesman gets past a certain door, there's no way he can sell anymore. So the salesman promises to cut someone into his downline if he helps him shift his last few batches. Tit for tat. This is an easy sell. He lifts his shirt - shows all the knives and their attendant damage. Lets the people in their safe warm homes marvel at the wound work. His colleague demonstrates a few samples, *"look how clean the blade is"* and *"you just don't get this kind of precision with your notoriety"*. The salesman breathing sharp, proves to eager buyers he knows blades. He knows blades so well. Look at what they've done to him. Don't you want to take part in this target practice? All so un-self-pitying. And they do. They ask if they can sell them too. The salesman smiles. *"Of course. There are always more knives to sell. More bodies needed to sell them."* More bodies to be found in. He will be rewarded, he is sure. Other salesmen's downlines are looking to the salesman for inspiration. No one has that high a knife to door ratio. They're all in. They follow his lead. Helping each other along as they go. They're learning community - more knives to sell means less stuck in them. But the salesman doesn't stop. He recruits a seller on every other doorstop. He'll get a cut of every sale. The whole town has knives now. Half are sellers, the rest, so impressed with the role knives can play in their lives, are fervent converts to blades. The town rewrites the history of knives, they're missing people by choice.

One of These Mornings
for Mario

Although my mother has died
she's alive in my dream, letting me
lean against the warm rock of her side,
resting her arm round my shoulder, gently
telling me *You don't have to die*. I wake
thinking about the black drag queen who sang
a bluesy *Summertime*, that sleek
white gardenia in her hair, lifting
her voice to glory in the room. Her visa
ran out. Letters drifted. The last we heard
she flew back home to South Carolina
and hanged herself. Was she scared
no-one would tell her *You don't have to die*?
Let her rise up singing and take to the sky.

My Husband in Hospital

I can't visit your ward. The pandemic
bars me, so we fall back on our phones.
It's your heart again, which means I panic
for your life. I mustn't be the man who moans.
Stay calm – it's not about me. I'm listening
to your voice. Does it sound breathless, anxious,
or relieved by the doctor's news, listing
good ways to get better in your gracious
syllables? I need a hug when you
say you've been hooked to a drip for six days,
six nights, to sort your blood. What's the view
from your window – is it hills, a sea-haze,
only clouds? There's so much I fail to know:
how your heart works, why we love, where years go.

Enough

The man beneath my skin itches to be out but is smart enough to know better. He's dumb enough to cut himself when no one's there, and numb enough to ignore the seep and scab. He looks through the holes in my face and shouts that enough is enough is enough is enough in the infinity chamber of bathroom mirrors. He's astute enough to know that no one's listening. The man beneath my skin is turning away, turning inward, turning into something more like a frightened child with holes in his face and no one there. His scabs itch and he will never be enough.

Legion

Though I view my gender identity like an astronaut in a long-running space opera views an ineffectual alien life-form from early in Season 2, I wish to be known as they/them to acknowledge the dissenting populace that buzzes beneath my skin. Think of a beehive with neither wax nor honey, or a football stadium with no game and no viable exits. Think of that shell of a planet in Season 8 with its core bored clean away. I wish to be known as spattered afterimages superimposed in primary colours as the ship jumps to lightspeed, my every face etched with dignified terror. Consider a museum of Noh masks, its walls folding into the origami of earthquakes, or Bondol's Apocalypse rippling into life in a fever dream. Remember the silent, green-skinned beauties from Season 4 as they dematerialised into cosplay, fanfic, and online petitions for their return. I wish to be known as all the nameless extras on union rates who were looking the other way when the cameras rolled that one and only time. Think about bulbs blowing one-by-one in an empty dressing room, or all the lottery tickets that didn't win big. Think about that pilot episode on VHS, lost to magnetic decay, or the shock cancellation when ratings wobble. They/them. All the gum cards no one collected. The dropped script concerning bees, beasts, and the illusory nature of linear time. I wish to be known. I wish not to be known. They/them/it.

At the Park, A Man, Sunbathing Alone

In a shallow dish of grass he had spread
his towel, white on green like football
chalk, and was now rubbing lotion
into his bald spot, his raw elbows, his shirtless
back. Meanwhile, June went on, all Hockney
yellow and blue, puddles of shade, birds
fresh from the egg, and the trees, passing
their notes, *do you fancy me Y/N*,
millions of cotton dates in the ice cream
air and this pink man, leaning down,
resting on his towel, cracking open
the afternoon like a drink.

Of Quicksilver
(after Robert Frost)

One year, at the caravan park
where my grandparents and I
spent part of each June, walking
and bathing in the sun and baiting
crabs with bacon, the owners' son
bought himself a telescope. He had
his own business elsewhere, I think,
outside of Barmouth, while his parents
kept watch over wild pigs and
old ponies and caravans.

One night, the son invited us out
to see through his telescope,
positioned on the grass above
the road lights and the scattered
town. He had my grandad look first,
who laughed and quietly scratched
his moustache, then left the lens
open for me, and suddenly:

the moon collected

into an intimacy I hadn't even seen
my own face; suddenly more than
some local name, this luminous pool,
silvering the night. I stared into it until
the telescope was shifted, to see Jupiter
and Mars, trembling in their earthy light,
but eventually the cold became as crisp
as water, my grandad had to take me inside,
and I tried to understand what it was
I should do with this full moon
resting underneath my eye.

Schoolboy Pressure

We stared as witnesses in the Science experiment,
fixated by a metre rule half-covered
by three sacramental sheets of newspaper,
the other half projecting like a diving board
over the laboratory bench.
None of us could press the ruler down,
laid in testament to unknown forces.
The corduroy teacher smirked and explained that
'atmospheric pressure' kept it in place.

Dad would tap the seaside b&b barometer
pretending he knew the scale,
like his counted strokes on the bicycle pump,
thumb and finger pressure gauge on the tyre wall.
On the day my feet could tip-toe the floor from the saddle,
new friends and feelings free-wheeled into frame
connecting all the lubricated chains and cogs.

I could sense a five-mile column of air,
amassing to almost fifteen pounds,
        on every square inch

    of tingling skin.

Study of a horse chestnut after a child has self-harmed

conical blossoms
more at home in the ocean
the peach inside each white petal resembles
the contents of a clam or mussel shell
or a merman's foreskin   the entire tree
a knackered chandelier on a sunken ship

davy-lamp-shaped flowers
ghosts of every jilted bride in folklore
too high to reach and pin on your lapel
or hold as a 99 without the flake as you watch
it melt and fall to the floor and receive a slap
on the back of the legs and not have it replaced

I count them all to pass the time on the upperdeck
knowing it's not long until the spikes
and collisions come

Finding Dad in the Racing Pages

1   drizzle   **HE ONLY CRIES** softly in coughs............................**on the phone**
2   stop   **WHEN A DOG DIES** smoker's hack..............**whiskers scratching**
3   silence   **PARVO THIS TIME** disease on his boots............**brought it home**
4   ache   **EMPTY GREENHOUSE** arthritic knuckles.....**furlongs of fag ash**
5   growth **COMPOST BAG** carried like a corpse............**chair by the radiator**
6   glow   **PARAFIN HEATER** worked hard in winter......**reaching for words**
7   fence   **FORGOTTEN BIRTHDAY** a fallen jockey............**hope trampled**
8   listen   **WINNER AT DONCASTER** taken as a gift.........**crumpled paper**
9   gone   **TOMORROW'S BACK PAGES** daily call................**Daily Mirror**
10 last   **BOUND BY HORSES** what our love needs.....**a steward's enquiry**

Rabbit Stew

We trudged on home with heavy boots
and trousers covered in hay.
Lying face down in the hedgerow
for hours, grandad's beard held debris.
Lean conies, slung over shoulders,
the blood on their coats was black.
Sliced top to tail and turned inside out—
I started to turn cold as I was eyed by you
and I said go inside, but you spied
the neighbours mottled rabbit suckling
on dandelions. So, you ran and shouted
hide,
to spare it from the feel of my knife.

> All I could think then was
> > what you thought of me.

Be a Man

My father told me on my
thirteenth, when he was my age,
he played men's football, snuck
into pubs and smoked my grandfather's
cigarettes. He Struck me round the ear,
for calling my uncle a cheeky bastard.   *Respect your Elders!*

At 15 I lost my virginity—   *Go on lad!*
too young to understand that me and
her were half a millimetre of latex
between orgasmic ecstasy,   *Condom? Fuck that.*
and unexperienced care of infancy.
Too proud to care, and just shared
it all with friends at lunch.   *What do her nipples look like?*

When I was getting in clubs
I was sticking tabs on tongue,
and shotting Jager.   *Get it down you Zulu warrior!*
Taxi back to her place, walking
home before they wake,
leaving them on read.   *Top Shagger!*

Then I fell in love.   *Gay.*
Overnight I *knew* how to
treat a woman.   *She faked it most the time.*
Within months we had a
baby on the way
and rings wrapped tightly
on our fingers.   *Rest in peace mate.*

When my little girl was born,
I saw pride, fear, and euphoria
wash over me. She was kicking
and screaming, clinging to
my breast—

all I could do was cry.
I'd never seen anything as
beautiful.

*You'll have your hands
full when she's older pal.*

I thought it was *her* who made me
hate women.

Yeah fuck `em.
Unfit.

She left and took the baby,
so, I just swiped left and right;
trying to use someone for the night.

Smash n' Dash!

It didn't matter that one fell so hard,
when I went back to my ex,
she broke in half. I still think about
the hurt I caused her now.

Don't be fucking bent.

When it all got to be too much.

`ere we go.

I was given repeat prescriptions,

Weak.

not listened to by physicians.

Just football blues.

Went hungry—
£50 an hour
to learn to talk and listen.

Never gets the round in, tight cunt.

Jumped upon for
being unemployed.

She deserves a man who can provide.

Shut the fuck up!   You can't speak to a woman like that.

Anamia

Straight after dinner,
he tiptoes upstairs to his
cool, tiled sanctuary
and bolts the door behind him.
The ceremony is about to begin.

There's piss on the seat but the smell
helps him retch, spit-wet fingers
tickling tonsils to trigger the purge -
an acid backwash of food twice-tasted,
rotting the teeth from his head.

Saturday

The world is a wet street. People step between puddles
that haze with spray. In the pub, no one moves.
Umbrellas drip by the door, windows steam. Time is a pint
that will not drop. At the end of a road, past the pouring eaves,
the sun falls gold on a new estate. It shines bright
and false, like some risen town washed from the deep.
A redbrick Atlantis, where the men sit quietly with papers
and read about sport, or tinker in a shed with tools and mowers.
Not lost in a car park, searching. Walking from space to space,
model to model. The key fob fired like a desperate flare.

Chameleon

You would believe, watching the way
he strokes the chin of his pet

chameleon, that this soul
knows nothing about torture

or tying a drug dealer to a chair
and leaving him for days.

When a chameleon changes colour
it mimics the surrounding

palette, blending into brick or leaf,
prey or foe. What skin

would you take
on this estate, with that father?

baby oesophagus crow

i search netflix for miserable movies to cry to.
my wife tells me i listen to too much depressing music,
falling escalations of clawed, corvus notes —
my heartbeat's drum.

my brother sighs when i get a story published,
'who dies in this one?' & i ruffle but never tell him
it is always him, one way or another.

& my father asks why i can't write something happy,
just something happy, & inside i caw, my bones bellow,
my feathers rustle as i reach for the wine.

i do not wind-slap the bottle & smash it to the ground,
purple staining the white clouds of his memory,
do not screech at him because you left,
because you always left & when you came back
you were never really there.

do not yap about mum's medicinal concoctions to sleep
away that feathered darkness inside of her.
do not talk about that closed window
i beat against time & time again.

instead i squawk that happiness is already understood,
understandable, it needs no beak, no beady eyes,
but the harrowing moments need petrol vestments
& crumbs to pick at, or some kind of crow shit answer
to make him think i am intelligent.

& i dare not mention the many times my brother has tried
to take his own life & how every call i receive in the night
is crow's covetous cackle

brother's dead, brother's dead, brother's dead.

so i find miserable movies on netflix to attach my hooked, crowed grief to
but still only write about death & sadness & those moments in between
which nobody tends to notice.

seeing my dad in his underwear

my mum in hospital, finding breathing
hard. my dad asleep in bed

reaching out to my mum's side
only to find nothing.

he wakes with the click of the door
& says, Barb love, is that you?

shadows though there is no light. when
did he become so old? a museum of defects —

his baby toe curled the wrong way,
eyebrows falling to his face. his mouth

trying to smile, his skin rough as a leaf.
& my own grief, what to do with it,

how to keep it curved, soft as lace.
& all the phone calls I cut too short,

how will I get that time back
to say, no, no, I'm not busy,

go on, tell me all about it.

Blue Paint

It had sat there at the back of the shed,
only once used for an overcoat, then left.
The lid slipped but had never been tightly fixed.
In truth, it dropped and fell through me.

It oozed into the cracks of the wooden floor.
Thick, undiluted, sludge-like, it moved across
and onto my hands as I tried to reverse
its flow back into the fallen tub.

Evading my attempts to stop it spreading,
it made its way into the house,
marked the sides and base of the sink,
sealed into the pores of my fingers, palms.

Only then did I notice that you had it on you too
as you crawled in from the garden
where you'd played with Buzzy Bee.
Subtle streaks signed off on each arm.

You cooed and babbled, oblivious
to the new bold highlight of *Blue Sky View*.
Not one of the toys even had a fleck mark.
You were careful enough to protect them.

It would take an age to wash it off;
fading slowly, unapologetically.
Though you smiled, I winced, knowing
this stemmed from what I'd failed to grasp.

Habitat Analysis of a CD and Record Fair

Shunned by those that search the cloud,
for us, the last of a tribe, this is the sweet spot.
No one disrespects the man at the door
who nods to a tune only found in his head.

We try not to show that we've noticed
his Pixies T-shirt is peppered with holes
and stained. A free-spirit, he looks nonplussed,
stamps our hands, goes back to nodding.

Inside, sounds compete for airspace:
drum 'n' *bass* booms over Elvis,
blue-grass dominates electro-pop,
punk is overlayed by a burst of dub

that shakes the town hall, each timber of it,
as if it were an ear-drum. Traders lip-read prices
as middle-aged men riffle feverishly
through crates of tatty LPs. The smell

of BO ensconces these taste-setters of their day
and the release of pheromone unites them
in the same way they are united by the hunt
for the best theremin, hook or reverb.

A group of younger Goth/ Emo/ Metal sorts
are harder to categorise and are keen to explore.
They flex their leather trench-coats,
like discerning fruit-bats by *Industrial/ Experimental.*

In the *New Wave* section, a lad with a Mohican
but still in his supermarket uniform,
holds a rare promo aloft, as if it were the answer
or at least a winning lottery ticket.

A speaker blows before the good bit.
We gather as one, punters and traders alike,
to gaze at the ruptured sub-woofer
as if it's an animal that's died.

Not to be published poem 1

I am a white man. I had cannabis psychosis for two years and
my mother is my friend. When I run I see shards of black
in my vision from a loosely detached retina
because when I was eighteen I thought staring straight into
the sun would fix my head. I used also
to turn round to see if I could see colours
rushing to reach the edges of my field of vision.
My mother screamed
at me and I remembered when we used to
lie in bed together and press our faces
and hands together before I fell
asleep. I didn't have memories of a time
before that, except sitting in a
converted fireplace and looking out, my mother
looking in, and other times when her desperation
was too much and I mocked her. I stayed
for eight years with a partner who read my emails
who I thought I deserved as punishment from a deity I knew
was not there, that filled the part of my head
that fell almost entirely out when I was eighteen. I sweat
from medication and I am not sure what music I like. I am not sure where
the centre of my mind is. Sometimes I feel
a trickling, slow and deep beneath my scalp,
not a metaphor
for anything.

Not to be published poem 2

...while in their skulls, to crown their discomfiture, a pelting of insatiable blows.

— Samuel Beckett, *Mercier and Camier*

I sleep with the violence and rise with the violence. I am with the violence and of the violence. My throat sings with the violence. I howl with the violence. The violence reaches through me and compresses me. I assume the dimensions of the violence. The violence crushes me as it courses through, a pelting in the skull, a plume about the skull, a spouting from the skull: the violence of scale, of girth, of timbre, the violence of texture and touch, the violence of scuffing shoes, the violence that slew villages, knew conquest, the violence fattened on grief, pumped through the eye of a needle, spewing between sharp white teeth, knowing nothing of itself, slick, vacuous and horrible. The violence engulfs me. My lungs blossom in red. The violence thickens into speech, the quickening, the setting, the pickling of the violence, the speech of a violent man, the shirt and trousers and girth of a man, a man, not a man, not a man, get that man away from me.

And the Dark Goes Out

I can't forget
how you looked through me   that night
your lips corrugated by words
you didn't know how to say
till they slipped from your mouth
like fluorescent eels

You're a bit _____
but manly enough not to worry about it

Proof! I didn't screech
when your fastball hissed at my eyes like a meteorite
I didn't cry when my frenemy   Elio
purpled my mandible with feldspar knuckles
I didn't flaunt Mum's swish capris on the street
till Halloween   when I was masked
in the face of a psychopath from a slasher flick
I didn't pout in the mirror
with black tears melting pyroclastic
Except when I did
the whisky on your breath
whispered for a kiss
and I said *Not me Not me*   *Not ever*

Swimming With My Ex at Man O'war Beach

I giggle electric through collapsing waves
while his fingers   chew   on my shoulders
squeeze me into his bristled chest
I'm bream-slick in a hero's grip   *hold still!*
smile! I fade out to Christmas
and unwrap a photo of me slung in his wolfkin body
his head lolled over mine   dripping
threats that click in my innermost ear

now the underhouse vault

where he pins me on the splintery table

lamps haloed on his hair like beneficent Virgil

coaxing me

through the seventh circle   of ~~heaven~~

ssssst!   I reappear in the riptides
and battle to shore in a rented
body   skiff of driftwood   sun-irradiated
crashing   years later
into the fractal of my therapist's eye
a dark through a whorl of sapphire opens
to howl my shame

Joke Research

Take any cohort of [ten or more] men
in a pub in buoyant mood
and drop a joke about women.

There's a surge of laughter – but listen:
There'll be one amongst them at least
whose tone is somehow in earnest

and while at closing most move on
to mothers, sisters, friends and lovers,
one leaves validated, pensive, alone.

My First Year Abroad: Selected Texts

Text 7
Again there's 3 or 4 of them on the tram,
cool eyes fixed on me
out of mannequin-still features
that the jiggling over tram tracks won't shake
into anything resembling emotion
and that's why I'm texting you – I mean
the men here, they're hard as nails
and I daren't look up from my phone here.

Text 8
And there's the women too. They gaze
right at me, into my eyes, but somehow
without passing deeper. Those cool eyes
from mannequin-still features – Help!!
I've fallen in love 5 times
on the way to work already
(but I don't know what, let alone who with).

Text 73
BTW I can report re. those stares
that no, the men are not hard
and no, the women do not find me
superficially irresistible: au contraire my friend.
It was me all along, carrying
my English male head into a culture
it could never have understood off the bat
and off the bat getting it all wrong.

Text 74
No No No Mate! I didn't get it either.
It's like this: here they just look at people
like they might a passing car
that ignites a passing interest

on a tired morning train journey.
They are so at ease with other people.
They are so NOT hard.

Text 137
I'm beginning to find the courage
to look at them too – to look at people.
Even to look at people looking at me.
It's thrilling – but not in the way
it was back home mate.
I'm never going back to that mate.

At the Buffalo Irish Center for St. Patrick's Day

when this drunk older woman comes up to me and rubs my chest
"Strong bones, go fight Putin" she tells me
with a thick Eastern European accent

she's from Poland, married to some Southtowns cop
we talk about the war as teen girls in curly wigs
dance on the ashes of empire

afterward I'm alone in the parking lot
plucking out my chest hair one by one
scattering them on the chainsaw ground

where they transform into gummy worms
slithering down Abbot Rd looking for paradise
it scares me what will happen

when they return to my body and the sweetness is gone

Carl Bangs on My Car Window Asking for Money

and I have a whole bunch of change
in an empty pack of Marb Lights
so I give him that
like a maraca he shakes my addiction with his addiction to make sure I'm
telling the truth
when he walks away a symphony slinking into the shadows
Bidwell Pkwy a minefield of receding hairlines
the heifer hum of a city about to be born again
we just don't know what it'll look like
nights like this there are mountains of eyelashes
getting blown apart by the wind
we've been plucking them out for what seems like forever
the belief that wishes have a better chance at coming true
if we gather them together

Heart / My father paints my bedroom / Hand on Heart

I've spent too much time narrowing grief
over anger. Afraid my silhouette, masculinised

looms over a cat's orange paw print – crisp
on the white sheets covering the furniture.

That my broad hands violent rattling
of a child's bunk bed frame is somehow inevitable.

At some point I inferred that the trade off
for anger was a chocking heart. That the hands

our father's bequeathed us grip our arteries
applying a small amount of torque.

But those gifts aren't ours unless we take them
and if we do, we choose how we keep them.

Crying Diary

Three times today:
When I pushed a trolley past happy, pink Her Birthday cards and looked away;
When I saw a film I knew we could share and wanted to phone you;
When I listened to one of your crackling records,
wondering what song might have been your favourite
and knowing I couldn't hear you sing it.
Twice today:
When I booked a train to Brighton because you'd said I'd love it
(was this your last holiday?);
When someone talked about cancer on TV and it sounded different than before:
an unwelcome relative.
I only cried about you once today:
When I was happy and then remembered you were dead.
Three times again today.

Possum, Drowning

It is the most natural thing in the world to leave, so leave and take your sourdough with you. It gives me the shits. I hate being alone more than I hate being with myself, so I'll suffice. The things we make make us sicker and more miserable than we were before, unless we make a mess of things, then we'll have each other to hate. I have made a mess of loving myself, I have made a mess of my sleep hygiene. Is it hygienic to sleep inside of a ballistic missile? The night crawls on and a dog dies nearby. I feel bad about it but do not cry, cannot cry, am too much of a scumbag to cry. A man stands in the road with a shotgun. He is not my father, so we tell each other we love each other. What I would do for him to be my father, or two moths dancing in the cold sky. The moon will kill the poets eventually. The snow will turn the dead of December over, gifts for the ever-violent Claus. There are more cops in this world than dreams. There are no accidents, only the end of everything; the first time I ever told a man *no* was when I took his gun from him.

Rent-A-Prick

Isolation is a domestic task we   prove
yourself worthy of solar systems and
endless arrays of space   time
to waste and time to kill my   self
centred and an asshole, then what are you?

I am mundic, this house is falling   apart
of me in every obsession. If I am   made
a cake, baked myself into it, ate my   own
up to our faults or live in this   state
my intentions before I pull the trigger.

Seriously, I taste great as cake, all   cut
up angels and a back catalogue emo   record
yourself hating yourself and play it   back
to back in a barn with a guy your mate
recommended for intensive therapy.

Every time I've considered giving   up
yours, I've never seen a cry for help I didn't   love
me in ways your dad never loved your mum.
We're all skin and bone but some of us have
a reason to power through the hayfever.

Ashley is in the gym right now

Ashley is in the gym right now
and has forgotten his legal visit.

Ashley's contempt creeps around the closed door
of the booth and settles in the empty seat.

Ashley's recently-used disinfectant
reeks up and down the corridor.

Ashley's snigger at the pink wristband
his visitors are given by the prison
winds around the chewed biros.

Ashley's unlaundered uniform
is warming another bench somewhere.

*

Ashley's bare lightbulb accepts
that the substance of what it was said that he did –
that he threw a kettle of boiling water
in his cellmate's face one morning when they said
his mum sucked dick back in Kingston –
was basically true.
                              Ashley's acceptance
gathers in beads;   runs down the walls.

Ashley's absent muscles flex
either side of the air, across the table
from both members of his legal team.

Ashley's ticking panic light
asks what he should have done, just sit there and take it,
just take it like a little bitch,

you think he should just sit there and take it like a bitch,

would you let someone say that about your mother,
for real, would you just let someone say that?

Ashley's legal team do not say what they would do –
   Ashley is in the gym right now –
and instead draft letters to the Court and plead
for one more extension on the case deadline
for a client who is not being cooperative.

*

Ashley's unopened cell door drums
the end of British Summer Time.

Ashley's unopened case file fills
the air with whispers of extensions denied
over Christmas. Ashley's eyes close

as he pushes dead weight of the day away
for a moment, in the gym, right now.

Andrew Tate is Not Afraid

there are people out there who want you to be helpless / they want you to be cowed and submissive / because then you're easier to control / they want you to believe there's a crisis in modern masculinity and you know what there is / and that's your opportunity / because crisis and opportunity are the same thing / in fact in japanese they're the same word

what i'm here to tell you is that you are in control of this crisis / your thoughts shape your reality / you have seen a tear in the fabric of the matrix / there are people out there who don't want you to know that / they will try to take your power / and those people should scare you / they don't scare me / but they *should* scare you / because fear and strength are the same thing

and there are all sorts of things that i *could* be scared of / except i'm not / like sharks / and tigers / and russian chess masters / and people who are very animated when they talk / like me / i move my hands all the time / because being animated makes you more capable of assassination / i'm not a violent man / but crisis and masculinity are the same thing

and the concept of love / both the actual concept of love / and the 2002 hideki naganuma song of the same name / and electronic music generally / any music that holds the possibility of dance / because dance music is poor people's music / and if you're poor you have to get close to one another when you dance because the basements where they party are so fucking small

and getting close to other men / especially men with torsos glowing the hot light of some tiny fucking basement somewhere where nobody is drinking sparkling water and where these people move their hands all the time / getting close to those men is *terrifying* / i'm not scared of it / but it is *terrifying* / because terror and desire are the same thing

and getting close to women / especially for sex / sex is boring / frankly / boredom / boredom should scare the fuck out of *everybody* / because if you're bored then you start asking stupid fucking questions / and how are you ever supposed to be free in a world of slavery if you're always asking stupid fucking questions

and finding that small tear in the fabric of the matrix and stepping through into a world where not only do i *look* like the rapper / pitbull / but i *am* the rapper / pitbull / and people keep getting the two of us mixed up / and keep asking me to play this stupid fucking poor people music in poor people parties in poor people basements / and they're not even wrong

a world where people watch movies other than the matrix / where people don't care about sparkling water / don't care about the size of the basements where they dance their fucking dances or listen to their fucking songs or read their little fucking poems on and on into the night / a world where love resides

that world should fucking terrify you / because terror and desire are the same thing

Moonchild

Everyone is a moon.
— Mark Twain

A man, full of sea waves, is learning
to swim. To breast-stroke between
the twenty-nine words for sorrow;
to unpace the halls of haste.
Stay afloat, my black water cat!

Two habits ago he unchained himself from the moon
while listening to an eternity's monody.
The eye of a candle
through electromagnetic darkness.
Undercertainty.

Who splash-hops past us
treading on drowned monuments' heads?
Who sings *Bye-bye, gravitational pull*?
No weather here.
No need to read a hairy map.

The beach, a grove of flutes... The man is
an embryo inside a light bulb.
Shining is within.
His *intos*, *been-throughs*, and dark *ifs*...
The feline eye of an old radio...

Only the Boldest Utopians

Man learns to be a kingdom; he admires
whatever populates his parliament brain.
He goes to the esplanade, looks at the women:
the guilty ones are the best.
Is guilt our new commodity?
How poor are the pure?

Man wills his wildest; man craves
alchemical bliss. Beauty,
only visible from within.
Authenticity bride ignites her bra candle.
Ambiguity plucks the air guitar.
Genetic faults smell like protoplasm.

Man attempts to husband success.
Is he marrying aggrandisement?
Will he go a-traitoring, slow-donkeydly?
A church is a walk in solitude. Scuffed up
into a duty, the simplest of theocracies.
Lightning never strikes in a vacuum.

If Smart Bombs Thought like Men

I wait alone, under the earth.
I have played the waiting game
for many, many long years.
I wish to be free.

Flying high above the land.
Flying at the edge of space,
So high I could kiss the stars,
but it is the ground I will
embrace when I fall

spilling forth my bounty:
Heat, energy, neutrons
gamma rays, caesium
strontium and above all
such a beautiful burning

melting steel, shattering
concrete, turning sand
into glass and flesh into
ash and shadows.

That is the future.
Now I wait in the dark.
It is so unfair.
I have so much to give.

My time will come.

Ode To Jockey(s)

Beside the pairs of light
and dark blue jeans,
an entire shelf was dedicated
to the gleaming torsos
of white men. In the only
affordable mall,
my family would spend hours,
afraid they might miss
something On Sale.
It was our monthly pilgrimage
where desires were cheap
enough to place
in the gaping mouth of the
rolling carts and that too
without any shame.
Away from the prying eyes
of my mother, I would
orbit the aisle that displayed
the many forms
of similar men, all willing
to smile down at me,
their bare bodies made
glossier by the lights above.
They were what we called
in school Hollywood Men,
the objects of every
girl's fantasy. If somebody
were to take a notice,
they would have wondered
what a kid of 13 wanted
from a section made
for bodies larger than his.
I didn't want anything
except this feeling

in my stomach like I had
swallowed sleeping butterflies,
now awake and fluttering
to find a way out.

The Ark

In a Catholic, all-boys, boarding school,
The dormitories should surely be
Named after saints, revered past abbots,
Roman colleges, Old Testament books;
At least, perhaps, nearby Berkshire parishes.
But we had "White", "Brown", "Blue," and "Open,"
This last holding 40 or so boys' beds *en masse*;
I think there was 'Upper,' maybe 'Junior,' too.
But notably then, 'The Ark': single cells,
In a redbrick, three-storey rules-coffer,
A large, flat-bottomed boat, in which
Sixth-formers ride out God's vengeance,
With their porn mags and black-market blocks of fags,
One-by-one.

Blind Jack

Play the field, then elope with your sweetheart,
Save the drowning soldier at your 4th attempt;
Beat the Colonel in his coach back to Yorkshire on foot,
Mischance and adversity treat with contempt.
Play wily cards and fiddle with elan-
Have a way with people and skittish foals;
Escape capture at Culloden, recruit for the King-
Drive coaches in snowstorms on Pennine hills.
Have a glint in your eye and a ready wit-
Make a name for yourself, be a pioneer;
Trust what seems to your inner eye fit,
Build roads and bridges where others would fear.
Armed wi' nowt but nous and a doughty staff,
Be half the man that was Blind John Metcalf.

A Fantasy: One Day I Get an E-Mail

The worst thing that ever happened is the best thing that ever happened. Let me be more specific: one day I get an e-mail in my Junk folder and it says, "Hello I know your password" and then proceeds to yes, list an old password I once used to access my bank account. The message goes on to say that my computer has been infected with malware, and as a result the sender has full access and control over my computer: they know all of my passwords, can turn on my camera or microphone and I won't even notice it. Moreover, they have used this malware to spy on me via my webcam, and have recorded me satisfying myself. If I don't pay them $1200 of bitcoin, they are going to send this video to all of my contacts and post it on the web. Naturally I'm terrified. I screenshot the message and text it to Jackie, then proceed to call her. Is this real, I ask? (Jackie's really smart about stuff like this). No, she says, I don't think so – it's a common spamming technique. Just be sure to cover your webcam with tape and use private windows that do not track when you look at porn. It's good advice and these are the steps I intend to follow, but an interesting development occurs: I find I can't even look at porn anymore. I know, I know, you don't believe me, but it's true! I'm terrified that something or someone is going to catch me and film me and blackmail me and ruin my life. Days turn to weeks, I'm still not looking at porn, and wouldn't you know, the sex becomes incredible. My shaft is full-bodied; I'm like an in-season pluot, bursting and full of juice. Furthermore, my intimate actions turn tender and more conscientious. Even when it's rough, which has never really been my forte, it's rough in the ways we want it to be, not because I'm mimicking some move I saw on my phone in the bathroom thirty minutes before. And all this, of course, does wonders for the time we spend outside of the bedroom as well. I finally improve those listening skills I've always been meaning to address. Jackie becomes even more beautiful as she ages, like a Van Gogh or a Mirren. Decades later, I'm an old man with liver spots on the front of my head and tufts of white hair sprouting out of my ears, and we're still going at it. Like I'm literally in the geriatric wing of the hospital and when the nurses aren't looking, Jackie is slipping off her granny-panties then climbing aboard for one more ride. I have something to tell you, she says between elderly moans, about that spam e-mail you received all those many years ago. I know, I say, kissing her again, I know...

Taking Out the Trash

At my best friend's wedding, I noticed that
he – my best friend – looked exactly like a
younger version of his father. I'm talking
same face, same expressions, same slump
in the shoulders: the whole shebang was
identical. It occurred to me
that I must look like a younger version
of my own father, so I left the wedding early
and ran home to him – my father – who was busy
taking out the trash. "Help me with this,"
he said. I looked at his eyes, his hair, his
hands, everything. I saw myself in thirty-four
years. "Dad," I said, "does it get easier?"
"Does what get easier, m'boy?" he said.
"This life," I said, "this endless struggle to
piece together what we think will breed
happiness, ever knowing that the sickle waits
for those we love and us ourselves. Does
it ever let up? Does it ever get easier?"
My father shook his head and said,
"M'boy, the only thing that gets easier is taking
out the trash," and with that he grabbed
a plastic garbage bag full of empty bottles,
and threw it up into the air with all his might.
The bag flew over the rooftops of the neighbors'
homes, and over the roofs of the neighbors' neighbors,
and off in the far far distance we heard it
crash down onto the cement pavement.
It was an unbelievable sight, despite
the fact that with that throw my father had violated
every recycling code of the neighborhood.
"Dad," I exclaimed, "that was amazing!"
"Sure," he said, "but now I can't use my arms for a week."
"So everything has a price," I said solemnly.

"Shut up," my father said, "let's go inside
and watch Kung Fu: The Legend Continues."
Like we used to do, I thought to myself,
awake inside of the dream.
"I'm going to miss you," I blurted out, but
my father had already turned to go,
so my words landed where his shadow had been.
"Dad," I said, pre-grief, preparing.
"Dad," I called out again.

Versions of the Life Force [The Greyhound]

Not ghost not Agape not Abigail not object-of-prayer
but as much of cap and rosy sighthound vest you can see
as any hint of body between them you cannot
I am your jet black nails your lipstick scooper mauve
your jasmine your ylang-ylang your ambergris
your rouge your pluck your blusher says the greyhound
I am precious like plum sap like moly like calcium
more your state than the state of your condition
I am this version of grace this power this act
your gift your flaws your disorder says the greyhound
says the arched loin the dew-claw the bones
says the foot well-knuckled says the holy guttersnipe

Lab Sample 1: Espoliniq, Controlled Drug to Suppress Agitation, On Entering the Bloodstream

Jump at the outage of God   Jump at the voice in the voicemail
Jump at catkins   skin-tags   goggles   chlorine   Jump at bullfrogs
without teeth but with large hands   Jump at nude baby birds
Jump at small talk   dentures   tics   hair loss   the waves through the gaps
Jump at ringtones   tap-drips   roosters   split lips   ratchets   clocks
Jump at flyspeck   pier-stilts   Jump at your own nostril magnified
Jump at a view of the lane that seems to rise vertically and break
the laws of perspective like Chagall   Jump at centrifugal pump
Jump at creases   stethoscopes   hornets   the zippo in the coffin
Jump at nits   Jump at a hundred word sentence without a verb
Jump at the thought behind the thought   Jump at impromptu   Jump
at the thrill you feel when you are actually endangered   jump
at safeguard   jump at failsafe   jump at vouchsafe   jump
at protected from or not exposed   unlikely to be harmed or lost

Pops wants to be Grandpa

I've won awards,
I've made history,
neighbours wish I
was their son.

Bosses tell me
I'm great, focused,
rounded. Clients tell
me I'm a godsend,
I make things easy.

"You go!"
"Congrats again!"
"I'm so proud of you!"
"Keep it up, my friend!"
That's what people
comment on my social
media. I like the comments.

But when I go home,
the world feels like a
pessimistic poet. My
father keeps asking me
when I'll give him grandkids.
He wants them before he dies.

I Don't Have a Sister

My brother lives in another country,
miles, storms, reunions away from home.
He called mom last Thursday, crying;
snotty nosed, red eyes, sharp breaths.

Life's drudgery was crucifying his
shoulders, and the only hope he had
denied him three times, lashed him
aplenty: cheating wife, lost job, solitude.
So he crawled to mom and cried.

But there was no breast milk.
Mom told him to shut up and stop crying
because she did not raise any daughters.
Just two sons, and men don't cry.

Threadbare Man

I had just popped into the newsagents,
the old man was in front of me,
threads hung from his coat, trousers and shirt
like a homeless jellyfish, the urge to pull
was overwhelming, his socks were completely
worn through, cracked skin poked above his shoes.
He bought two small cartons of orange juice,
fumbled his way to the exit. The young man,
in the fine black coat, didn't see him - collision
was unavoidable and as he went sprawling
across the pavement, arms flailing, a bus passed,
his threads caught in the wheel, and he unravelled
in a whirlwind of spinning cotton, gone. A loose strand trailed
behind the bus as it rolled on.

The you I knew, but

your right hand looks like it has been driven over by a steam roller,
You stuff the knife into what's left of that formidable grip,
it is useful as a kind of shovel. But so cold.
That tattered glove you warm it with
Can you fix this Ewan?
You hand me the Braun 6000, I open the cover
4 years of stubble falls onto mums' carpet,
I stifle my oops, to reduce further cleaning stress.
After a quick brush and a few drops
of rancid sunflower oil we have
action. He takes it without a word
shaves where he sits.
Have you seen my stick?
Why is that thing there blinking?
Can you get the rugby on this thing?
Have we got any croutons?
Thanks boy (twice, once for coffee once for wine)
That was Monday's conversation contribution.
Giant incontinence pants, knees that bend the wrong way
and look likely to give out momentarily.
A pack of tissues a day, a whisky and ginger at six
No crusts, soft foods. How can you be you? Or
were you always, this?
It does feel familiar.
It's like you don't care,
you are just waiting, impatiently.
Not fading away but solid flesh with laboured breath.
Panting through these dragging quiet days, you disintegrate
like an abandoned anchor rusting at low tide,
a sandstone cliff slowly falling into the sea.

the world is hell, and men are both

though they ought not to be
        in this world, as it ought to be
with those devils nurtured inside
        the tormented souls are animals

        animals the tormented souls
they chop up — male chicks
        they won't breed — bull calves
won't eat grass — the ram lambs
        circle & circle — the fish
sleep horizontal — the trees

        crumble — the icebergs
so hidden-assed & wet eye-lashed — men
        without knowing this thing-within
is a thing-in-itself — unknowable but felt.

after Arthur Schopenhauer

Terry visits Burnden Park, 1977

I told him I was a Chelsea fan
as a toddler, I praised both ends —
worshipped Osgood and Bonetti,
harmonised that catchy blue tune.

More was his joy when he replayed
the seventy they injured on our ground.
Plotting their foray on the Intercity
to overthrow the Great Lever End,

police were diverted by a dummy squad.
Half-bricks picked from the Embankment,
they hormone-charged the length of
the grass — up & over our home fence.

I don't know who threw the rock
I ducked, or how close my ten-year old
lungs were to my last gasp, but I know
how much Terry loved until his —

friends were forgiven for anything,
which is more than can be said for
the others. Football was a matter of life
and death was the final whistle —

but nothing was loved like his laugh
— it still cackles in my head —
that time he lay half-asleep on the
vodka and I kissed his pursed lips.

i.m. Terry Fearn (1958-2022)

bruised male flowers.

when the beer slithers out of your father's hands.
it floods your home.
it soaks the walls.
and collapses everything.

what kind of flower
grows out of caved walls of a dying home?
if not a boy learning to make rain
out of bottles he saw his father shower in?
a boy watering himself while shedding his growing petals
in fear of the bottle reflecting him as his father?

if you watched your mother cut thorns
off her stem so your father can hold her,
and then watched him mishandle her instead,
force her to grow the thorns back in defense,
irrigate her with the poison of remorse
made of his hangover and recycled regrets,
what kind of flower would you be?
how many bottles will it take to water you,
to grow into nothing like him?

Responsibility

The kite flew across the sky-held moon.
Lifted by wind, guided by string,
gripped by tiny fingers.

Tyler let the wind stir him,
like honey into porridge.

He'd tied his Mum's fears at the end
of the pier. Her hoarse whispers:
How can I keep a roof over our heads
when I can't get out of bed?
How can I get help
when help is at the end of a waiting list
longer than I can hurt for?

Tyler had learnt that a cup of tea could not quench
her broken song's thirst.
But he'd discovered he could carry her weight for her
like a sponge absorbing water.

So, he stood before the nameless sea,
and offered his kite to the sky-held moon.

If I don't, who else will?

I, a man

I never mastered the art of being
a fist clenched around a stone.

I am a fist, holding
a balled-up love note;
perhaps all men are.

Trans Masculinity: The Journey Begins

what does the body say? my cheek panes, beardless, reflect
too much light: my hands seek rest from argument (motion repressed)
my lips regret each tender tendency—

> we are shriveled

animals

as my muscles break, my eyes rest as if never inhabited, or
my eyeballs blossom, rain through sockets, until water
exceeds light—

> father's fear, or mother's bitterness?

nature's complex: science grinds tranquility but my filthy life
paddles on: no coastline, no continent—

> to endure is not

proportion

I feel my dreams, muscled: my limbs are strong, my person-clay
reformed, my shirt torn from a superhero's chest—

> but disquiet

hesitates

in the breathless present, I can gnaw on bones, resolute, until
jaw rictus resolves, but
tastebuds, first-formed, are intricately worked—

> we are all intricate

sparks against window-shutters: I believe: if we can overthrow
impossible, we will find somewhere to live—

> a luxuriant room, a life

complete.

Killing It

perched on the bar   waiting for the latest
I see two lads   twenties   muscles   skin fades
tight tees   trackies   trainers   man uniform
they glug gut-filtered Guinness   wolf
pork scratchings   they bark about
how they're making a living by *killing*
it as British Gas salesmen   how they have
bagged girlfriends who are both dead
gorgeous   how they *own them   smash them   slay them*
yapping about lovers as if they aren't
alive   as if they're Porsches   piñatas   hogs
snorting about passion as if committing acts
of grievous bodily harm   homicide
about love lives in the language of death
my cheekbones turns up   a vision in denim
I tell him that *I am living for his new hair*

Steam Room

what brings you here

through red-lit steam

a straight hunk's voice in blue shorts

I want to lose my belly fat   tone up

on sweating walls the shadow of his head nodding

avoid sugar   don't eat past six   like me

a meaty hand pats pecs

I can't see his whole body in this darkness

would we even see each other

outside this room of steam

would we ever talk in daylight

on a pub garden picnic bench

Greater Anglia train

if we weren't stripped of our differences

Devotional for a problem of masculinity

I am a moving lump of cells that must follow certain rules. I
must be good with my hands, plane down wood as if I were a
pool attendant smoothing the surface of a lido. I confess that
sometimes I dream of my children dying and I will wake and
cry, but no one must know. Men don't talk about these things.
Last night my dead father came to me and told me he was
disappointed as what did I know about the spread of a virus?
He was not my father but some devil wearing his face as my
father was a good man. I try to live as him and I sometimes
fail, his hat too small, my driving more erratic. What quivery
pink cells I am on the motorway, shimmering in the fast lane
like the windows of a distant house at midday.

Devotional for fatherhood

We like the ruined castles. We can trace their shape in
minutes given half the chance. The smallest leads the charge.
I lollop on behind eyeing dangers he is yet to spot. The elder,
she takes the middle, pivots between us like a messenger
pigeon carrying news up and down the line. We pass older
people, they yield to us, wave us through as they grip the rope
upon the stairs. In darker corners, we play the game where
I am a hidden monster. I must still be me, but monstrous,
something recognisable and yet somehow undead. I lift my
hands and death-stare straight ahead, then catch them in my
arms and hold onto them as long as I can before they wriggle
free and leave me behind.

Boules

My brother wore our mother's wedding dress
on Halloween. His breasts were made of boules,
the brightly coloured plastic kind with water
that sloshes around inside to give them weight.

We walked the streets of Derry in the rain
until the dress' hem was black and sodden.
On Shipquay Street, a drunken stranger groped
my brother, slurring *Christ, your tits are hard.*

Reece Mews
for Francis Bacon

Small rooms concentrate the mind As a child
you were locked for hours out of earshot in a cupboard

Once your father saw you in your mother's underwear
holding your own adolescent gaze in an uncracked mirror

You never saw home again　　　*I'm not*
the sort of person who has vases

Bare floorboards, naked lightbulbs and whitewashed walls
freed you from the past's overstuffed rooms

The mirror smashed in a quarrel by a flying ashtray fragmented
your reflection into a glittering cobweb of eyes

We sat around on orange crates and a Boulle commode
Even a rug or a lampshade could have ruined everything

In a hotel room a body you have looked at many times
squats lifeless on a toilet　*My eyes are broken*

Seal the bathroom off from staff and let's continue
I have just bought the house I shall be murdered in

The books and photos and materials and clippings became a compost
lining the floor and offering gifts that glinted underfoot

Daubs and trickles congealed into a layer of guano on the walls
that the cleaner was not to touch　　Even the dust was sacred

Each item of this chaos has been catalogued and cross-referenced
Nothing is deader than the studio of a dead artist

still life with meadow flowers and roses

isn't this too easy? beneath the flowers
the men are fighting topless and bloodied
clutching the stems of each other's arms trying
not to be toppled trying to be the wind
the strongveinedleaves of their torsos curling
towards each other red poppies blushing
where they're cut beneath the fighters the flower
of a bruise beneath one thing another
beneath one man another man the floral
notes of gin (too much) above the meadowscent
of soil beneath one hand the neck beneath
the other hand the hole in which he'll plant
himself where the blooming will be hidden
held tight inside the tunnel the fingers helped to dig
one man wrapping his arms around the waist
of another whose limbs are drooping whose clothes
are scattered at the end of the bed and beneath
them both the salt outline of their temporary
life spreads towards the sun until the duvet
washes over them and they're gone

Quiet Boys Clean Their Plates

A corpse flower unfurls
in retrospect
Scented with the waft of
rotten years
All fattened and familiar

A linearity, but repeatable
Sick of these man shapes
carrying maggoty loads
around maggoty waists

We eat when there's dread
When ordinary things
are trussed up
Like Saturday liver
Mistrusted

My mother is dead to me
And still able to force down
forkfuls of fat into
my oesophagus

I eat when I'm full
At night and hidden
When I finger my paunch
Folding bread like a gag
Like all good boys should.

Tomorrow, I Will Take Care

In the dip before dreams
I repeat that tomorrow
can be loosened

Its incumbent chokehold
on roughening teeth
Peppered grey cheeks

Serum on edema
Release feet treacled in the
twist: maintain leanness

Sedentary positions are
unable to resist obscene
refrains

As each day rises like
a curdled sun
Say something to yourself

Gantries are prised away
As is time, as is excuse
Be a muscular derivative

Effortless distance runner,
to *'become'* is antithesis,
excessively realised.

Camp

Most likely Bulldog, undoubtedly something
brutal

and British, though with no real struggle
or stress for me, except

in my effort
not to get from the middle of that makeshift pitch

to its edge, but for a second
to look up...

               breathlessly. Everyone else

roaring by, but I
stood icon-still, knowing I'd been chosen

for one of my first important scenes— so small
among the big kids, oblivious

to heft and speed, but banking
on the kind of grace and fortitude

fuelling those slow clouds in that blue, blue sky

Tebori

No petal of moon
    glides this

ink pool. A sky

  blinking itself
    out of itself

   twice

   over the land

  when two bloodless clouds

swallowing stars
    uncurl
      to surface

      like ice-pale koi
  at the shadow of his hand

Bloody instructions.

1.

Class, paint in your books
using words alone. Conjure
for me what you can.

They summon dark clouds,
daffodils, long piers jutting
into lakes, the names

of birds, warm places...
sometimes knuckles, tears. Mostly
it's just *I*. As in,

See me. I was here.

2.

Year 10 are studying Macbeth's flaws.
I talk with them about dark, silent
ambition, the madness and the death
from murder and betrayal, how violence
has soaked our history, just how *forever*
this will need to be taught. We talk fluently
about the nature of people; whether
we all have the capacity for cruelty;
how this desire has shaped the world we live in.
I assure them that this is not the case.
We are all basically good. If you see someone
hurting then you help them, right? Thoughtful faces,
nods. *You love your family and your friends*
so you help them, right? A flurry of nods.

3.

It doesn't happen often. An average day
is lessons and books and *writing quietly*
and *well done for working hard*. It is the same
snatched chats in staff rooms and quizzes from lonely
children unsure of where best to *be*
during their *free* time. But when it happens,
more often than not the choir of "*fight!*"
comes first. And then the running, the slapping
of feet on playground concrete or hard
corridor floor and it grows to a stampede
crescendo. Perhaps a ruler was borrowed
but not returned. Perhaps someone said that
someone said that someone said that before...
Regardless, the origin will remain obscure.

4.

Hearsay whirls like swarming bats, rumours charge
through the halls like boars, fists will thump
like heavy toads in ponds of gossip, and hard
fact will relent to magic, all trust
settling in the dust of thrown words.
I've had students swear to bloody-knuckle
pummellings, hair-torn tearings, shirt
free ring sides, fractured teeth, hour-long scuffles
and bones splintered in a twenty child *rage
in the cage* death match. The reality
is teachers taking statements, tempers raised
in self-defence, red-faced thoughtless bullies
blushing in realisation, wiping
another's blood from their forehead, crying.

5.

They're very poorly
socialised this year. You can
really see lockdown...

They just don't know how
to interact. We've got to
teach them to be friends...

It all kicked off on
social media this weekend.
Today's been bonkers...

God help us when they're older...

*them boy

hatch from black bin bags in
back lanes. them boy

hear cries from abandoned
prams. them boy

hold cigarette campfires upon
metal stairwells.

hold the sirens in their fingers
at birth. them boy

hug the night. night hugs them
boy in grime. them boy

head to the riverbanks. become
fish gilled. gasping. them boy

head back to the towers. find
their tribes from the terraces.

hurl spit. one by one. the same
spot on ground. them boy

hang by bossman's shop. their bikes
like boys of their own. them boy

harvest the last bits of skin
on chicken bone.

hide their smiles under beef
stew pots.

hook tongues towards teeth. keep
them from being twisted. them boy

hate the silence. absence of news
is absence of   them boy

hum requiems from church pews.
just as their aunties do. them boy

hollow
                them boy

hand back the matchbox. let hands
weave them into wicker men—*

Common

A golden shovel after Dave

Football cages are solitary confinement for boyhood grief   Here you
grasp frozen air   Hear fractured tears drip from balconies knowing a body has dropped   Watch a single streetlamp dim   We're
taught street stains are unlawful   See graffiti   See litter   See all
blood stains as organic murals to those laid in the night   Alone
on curbs   Boys mourn around blood   Their hoodies pull faces in
gaunt   Nobody asks which face has passed on   They sense this
body dip often   Feel declining blips   Drop their breath   Together

I did not have chlamydia and was not pregnant, God bless

picture: i finish a vodka coke and the ice all in one. my mouth is full of ice. my tongue is numb. i'm trying to keep the cubes behind my teeth but dribbling all the water. let me be blunt, we left the club and i hold him in me like ice when it hurts, so alien that it hurts and its corners scrape your palate. i look ridiculous with how much i want and how often my body misbehaves. gets vampire-weird at night, wakes up to cause issues. a week later it's weeping every hour; i've eaten a bacon roll, pepperoni pizza, chorizo sourdough. ten years of vegetarianism down the drain, except for that time i ate crab sticks when i was on coke, but that was only once. i tell my friends: i am pregnant. Or i have chlamydia, no, i am not experiencing symptoms of either, but my vagina is being weird. i know i'm pregnant because my mother was a six-year-vegetarian and stopped because of her pregnancy cravings. feijoada heady with beef, melting so dark you can imagine your reflection. blood broth frothing, throwing up tender red bubbles like roe. pregos stuffed with steak - beat thin as a slip of skin. like coaxing back a scab, brushing the pink inside, pulling too far and coming back with a comet trail of better established flesh. no one should want so much, all the way from birth.

Not all men

Shut
the fuck
up
and listen

Trivial Pursuits

He that hath no beard is less than a man
— William Shakespeare.

"Have you always had a beard?" says the first person to see the sprouts of dark, overgrown stubble. He proceeds to obsess and mention my face for the rest of the evening. It reminds him of a guy he's dating.

"You look like Jesus" says my mum. I had to warn her half a week before she got to see it. She's been keeping this knowledge a secret from my grandparents – scared of their vengeance. By now, the scolding has become internalised. Even from half the planet away and two decades on, their reach is immortal.   Transcendent.

"You look like you've just gotten back from a gap year" says Conrad. He goes on to imply that I've become some crystal-collecting, weed-smoking pseudo-monk using my parents trust fund money. He then does an impression of a tory, which is slightly too convincing. His own facial hair has been stuck in stasis.

I glance into the muddy green irises of Emily hoping to see a glimmer of anything. But there's only emptiness and she tells me nothing.

She always preferred me shaven clean.

In praise of quiet boys

who house oceans inside them
greek fire burning atop emerald water

who hold so much loud in their hearts
angry pain that could bring cities
down in complete destruction

no body spared

in praise of quiet boys
who've broken so many noses open
clenched fists never swung

who in their mind
always have a perfect comeback
boys more than their darkness storming

these boys are siphons of masculinity
the kind you'll never find on streets

these boys are more than their quietude
the kind that speaks volumes

hand in form of mouth

Abuelo, a man of silences

My grandfather sits quietly
alone in a pew unsure if
morning mass has begun.

My grandfather sits quietly
in a living room of language
and laughter not his own.

My grandfather sits quietly
in an outside house he built
so that he might cry softly

long into the midnight hour.

My grandfather brews in sadness
at my dying grandmother's bedside,
sarcoma's violent alchemy at work.

My grandfather sits lost in thought
as I am fixed by his side, kneeling,
trying to surface a perfect phrase

wrestling our forgotten tongue.

Abuelo, a man of silences,
listens to his grandson
finally say *I love you*

in every language
we (n)ever shared.

Love Between Men

This is the way
I remember the shapes
that your mouth makes
when you try to say
words you can't say.

This is the way
your tongue and lips move
and the way this
imperfect language
is perfectly you.

This is the way
you've never been able to say specific.
You make it wide,
like the ocean
past the fence
past the flower surrounded house
that you built.

This is the way
you can't say flowers
but love flowers.

This is the way
I couldn't cope
when I realised I was broken.

And this is the way I moved away.

And this is the way
you said you weren't crying
— you just had
water in your eyes.

And this is the way
you didn't even try to dry
those eyes,
and how I cried, at last,
and how I didn't even laugh
when you tried to say specific.

This is the way you say
you don't speak good England
because England — like me —
is half a world away

past the house
and the flowers
and the fence
and the ocean
that — like you, yes, fluent you —
is pacific.

Enjoy Your Pint

At the bar,
in an unknown part of Birmingham
I bought two pints
and paid with paper money
from the northern part of Ireland.

That's not British money,
the publican said.
And I said, yes it is,
you'll see the royal head
if you hold it to the light.

And a man standing right beside me
turned to me and looked and said
So you're from Northern Ireland.
He was wearing
denim jeans and a denim jacket,

tobacco fingers fixed around a half drunk pint.
He locked his eyes on me and
moved so near I could have kissed him,
Whose side are you on, son? he whispered
Whose side are you on?

And I didn't know the landscape of belonging
in this part of England.
I hadn't seen signs enough to know
whether his hope flew for
the orange or the green.

He continued staring.
He kept right up close.
And I said
I hope for
peace.

And he said
That's a clever answer,
son.
That's a very
clever answer.

And I said
I know.
Enjoy your pint.
And I
got up to go.

Giant

My father was made in the lathes
his swarf scaled arms levered us to sky
he was born from stars of anvils.

My fathers shed was a second home
Where trees became tables or gliders
Blossom would envy chisel and plane.

In factory fortnight all the kids became giants
upon our father's shoulders dethroning sky
watching men go mad and pink in the sun.

Each Christmas day my dad slept all afternoon
my mum said it was the factory killing him
my dad said it was the turkey
I think it was the life
becoming his death.

Instructions on how to assemble a man

There is nothing romantic in love –
my old flatmate loved Bushmills
he drowned in its rotten glens
on the night he was alone
when thoughts stayed
and all he wanted
was Star Trek
and dizziness
and hard sex
as Dublin
vanished
outside,
inside
him.

The problem with men is manliness –
a blooding from birth continuing
from school fights to workplace
to being the man they wanted.
Men are very efficient killers
they do it to themselves
making the city limits
to becoming soldiers
then civilians again
but never the same
boy who dreamt
of becoming
happy and
enough.

SCRATCHATTHAT

he shivered and felt the skin on his arms get tighter inside the found jacket
that was stained and damp he thought it might be best to walk for a while
so he could make the time he needed on the schedule he had set but that
had lapsed into a series of grubby interludes and captured seconds of
intimacy under hesitant lights and abandoned heralds it was like being
trapped inside a grey bulge that was leaking into the bloodstream of
every complacent eater ordering treats behind glass under the pretext of
preserving the integrity of the averred purpose to persist on roads that
swerve without a threat manifesting he had been on the waiting list for
the trials and he had made the trip knowing that this would be the motion
which secured his designation as the bearer of the most advanced stage
of deterioration of all the potential subjects he bore the most prominent
distention his swelling inspired the light to fly from his face so that it was
refracted and the skin was always rippling with what was underneath the
constant industry of producing the bulging pockets that slapped with
every footstep he could feel them doing their work and he knew they
would break through before he made it there

Desire | Dad Bod

Put you in my house
– John Lee Hooker

Tonight I found my collarbone's drum note | a sharp
tap and it throats like a tom tom | the sternum drops
an octave | some gap perhaps | behind the lung
| an intercostal misstep | makes thunder | if you like
I'll play myself for you | one evening when
our blood's up | our daughters quiet or asleep |
our daughters who don't know their separate
bodies' borders | still too young | they share selflessly |
what age does the body become something else | synonym
like it is for us grown-ups | isn't it | tell me | when I give you
this | my body | when I talk my body to you | whisper it
to your eager ear | am I saying my body as it is | is it this body
that reaches you when I give you my body to hold | how much
arrives of what falls through the world | observable
at the mirror | it's foul audience | things bubble up | bad end
of a hair follicle | ingrown and coaxed with tweezers | red swell
at the jaw's thin flesh | when you see me look at you
do you clock the splodge on my eyeball | an egg
gone over | or my narrow bridge | oily T zone | if I eat
too much sugar it all peels | I'm not attached to it | this body's
reluctant tenant | these hairy allotments | but you place it
in your hands | clutch it | say you like some parts
like the thighs | one's scarred from a football stud
caught at twelve years old | three-inch ragged ladder
your fingers climb | time piece | shiny cicatrix |
there's another nick inside the wrist | site of a bone-pin
after I broke it drinking whisky at fifteen | a tiny star
fresh when we met | remember | this body at sixteen |
puppy fat balled on its smooth chest | once
struck a hardware salesman dumb | I asked
for a box of fifty mil countersunk | got ogled
in the warehouse | my hair gold and long
| I was called out in toilet queues | *we think you have*

the wrong line | *miss* | why am I saying
this | as point of departure | to show this body
has lied before | that people can be wrong |
but tonight I found my collarbone's drum note | play it
and the soft mammal opens up | is coaxed
to a run | shhhh | our daughters are sleeping | my hollow body
goes boom boom boom boom | ahaw haw haw haw

Desire | Running

The newest of the fathers are running | stiff
from anxious worry and running | running
until the fleshy drum of themselves hits
target pace | running hearts pump in the fathers
each morning | they gather water in a sling and
start running | anywhere they can | launched
sweating into the suburbs | running away from
and then back to their homes | they run until
they are filled or emptied with running | in circles
incrementally wider | running until they can run
harder and longer and further | this is stamina |
all of the new fathers run after all of the past fathers
| it serves an evolutionary purpose | they can't
stop | they are peaking | full of pain | can't throw
their conditioning away | they'll lose it all | there
are programs to follow | tell them what they must do
but still they worry | they must stretch and warm
up | warm down | worry all those ligaments | always
under impact | so they run until they find the zone
| use their bodies | hit the wall | they run at night
or in the grey mornings | they run until they are
finished | blisters and children biting at their heels

Birth Certificate (Counterquestions)

When the investigator arrives, I name him

here I am. I name him motherland. No one

will see you. I have given birth in the mirror.

A tatum, in all likelihood. Or Kokoschka's

sex doll. Ruptured and headless, of course.

Don't we name what we name to understand

what named us? The only truth is how water

speaks to the moon. What are we waiting for?

The more important the man, the sicker his sexuality,

wrote Alma Mahler. No one will answer you.

The committee. Between your questions, us.

Indeed. She wrote, *my fantasy is full of the most*

perverse images of cripples and seeking crippledom.

And did you get what you wanted? You are

never within, never without. Let me, too, be

an invisible act. Compassionate, selfless, yes.

What is between a doll and a pulse, a skin

and a lashing--this newborn and the next?

Saint (Strawberry Lemonade)

here at last the inscrutable city

is bound to be against you

the grass carries the weight

of your hunger it can hear

what's nearing a lie that feels

no guilt when it comes time

you are dancing everywhere

in your favorite song *all your dreams*

are made of strawberry lemonade naked

your image in the receding mirror

is what you hide from me things too

dark like breadcrumbs or horseflies

your mouth the color of memory

come here you say *no matter what is*

written on your t-shirt (SPITSHINE)

the whiteout on your finger is

barely dry the self-loading pistol

in your hot pants you bought

when you were a nineteen-year-old

saint putting clouds into a glass jar

I hold my breath as I wash your feet

as the black Mercedes S-Class pulls up

with the quarter moon remind me how

to erase myself kneeling in this green

The Landscape of Fear (A Duplex)

You don't need a million wolves running around to restore an ecosystem.
— Liana Zanette, University of Western Ontario

Walking by the hospital I ruminate,
startled by a lad-cub stomping his foot

       in my path. This cub, from a pack
       of lumberjack shirts who snort, pat

his lumberjack-shirted back. Little
protégé, unsettling his prey: setting

       down tracks, unsettling scent-trails,
       his howls bouncing off glass ravines.

At full-time, howls bounce like balls –
loud enough to fracture pint glasses.

       Lines drawn on these fractured paths:
       my thoughts scatter into dark cracks,

my silence spattered on their snouts.
Walking by the hospital, I ruminate.

Monolith

We met through *Rekt,* an app for famous
rectangles. The obelisk from Washington
DC kept messaging and as much as he
was virile, impressive, he's not even a real
rectangle. When he got all *Yeehaw* and
Masc 4 American Masc, I ghosted him.
The Rosetta Stone sent a voice message,
but we struggled to connect, even through
Google Translate. But with Monolith, I
guess I liked how mysterious he was, how
spacious. Sent me empty messages, until
something sparked like a reflected galaxy, a
door opening   We met at the planetarium
(obviously) - even though I had some
preconceptions, ie pompous sound-tracks
of Ligeti, or that I'd be expected to grunt
and go all Neolithic in his presence. We
found our silence really comfortable.
Sat in those reclining chairs with no star
show other than our reflections on each
other. Just the floor lights on the walkways
like landing strips, only the flashes of
romance (by which I mean comets),
reflected on that sumptuous surface: a
body you could just worship – a sense
of possibility on that radiant skin that
literally took my breath away. We stayed
there all night, but I won't divulge what
went on in those long, spaghetti-time
hours between dusk and infinity. We've
left things undefined, so as not to label
what we shared, or who either of us were
that night. We didn't swap numbers: why
bother, when I just need to close my eyes?

The Sun Also Rises

I was on the train from Lyon to Zaragoza and Ernest Hemingway was sitting next to me. We got talking. He made a similar journey, it turned out, almost exactly a hundred years before. From Paris to Burguete then Pamplona, for fishing and the fiesta. His train through France was so full of Catholics on some pilgrimage, he couldn't get a place in the dining car. He asked me if I'd ever seen a bull fight. I told him that the idea appalled me and he turned away to stare at the swampy edge of the Camargue, the lagoon at Sête, bright under the winter sun. He took out his blue-backed notebook and wrote in it with his pencil. Soon we saw a hint of the Pyrenees, some scrubby foothills, one high snow-covered peak. Writing, or the view, seemed to calm him. 'It's going to be a long ride, let's get tight', he said. Two bottles of wine later, we'd both relaxed. I asked him if he'd heard the one about the big game hunter and his wife.

Nicknames

Squeak and Nail came from what they brought in their packed lunches. Apple became Pip became Squeak. Chocolate Fingers became Finger became Thumb, which lasted most of a year, then Nail. Budgie had a beaky nose, and a surname that ended "butt". I've no idea where we got Grim from, maybe something he said one time. Squeak, Nail, Budgie, Grim and me. No way am I going to tell you mine. I expect everyone hated their own just as much as I did, but of course we couldn't say. Those names were how we told the others we loved them, or at least that we were happy to hang out with them after school, which for boys is more or less the same thing.

The Journeymen

For J.O.

We took the shrooms
in a field somewhere near Olympia

and walked
away from the music.

The doe we thought
wild

was a neighbor's pet.
I apologized to mint underfoot

and to you.
We shared pears

and dragged mummy bags
under stars.

The cold wanted to take me
and I almost let it.

We shuffled
through couches and women, sleeping

in the stands of trees
along highways.

My journals say I loved you. I didn't
tell you that.

If we had money, we split it
on tickets, on food.

Now she is leaving you, you say
on the phone.

There are broken Halloween animatronics
on the lawn

and the children
are not accepting euphemisms.

Consider school districts
and birth certificates and friends

with spare bedrooms.
How many nights in a tent too small

did we find gaps
the other did not need? I invite you

into the small square of earth
where I reside: supine

and sprawling, filling
into what is offered.

Lines on the Melodies in Men

It is funny I say to K, who's wading shirtless
in the burn, *the things we remember about growing.*
As a boy I played a game with my uncle
where I blew into his boxer's thumb
as he ballooned his muckle bicep,
the shoogly inkwork of his tattoos
smearing to a blur,
arms bulging bigger
with each puff I stuck him with
—stuffed solid as a cloud
before emptying its storm.

I blast another lungful down the thumb's
portal, slurp up the tobacco scum,
lick my lips like liquorice.
If they don't give it you my uncle gruffs
showboating his trophy muscles,
take it with these: a forced ending,
the cloven hoofed ars poetica
of Danish Harri—Da's toughest brother.

Popeye arms, I faked coveting them
knowing fine well
not even with a marching band
would I let that music in. It was
the haptic play I loved, the luminous
swell, like a kissing ritual
without the kiss.

The melodies in men are sometimes
my arch nemesis, a neighbour's
tusk, the wicked nimbus
of a better version gunning
for my soft & silly. Though mostly,

they're hot courage: brave bones stookied
in mucky fun, the buttress of friends
hatching bawdy superstanzas. Together
we might lay to rest our unclings'
bedraggled sermons, their: *just
a generational thing, a not in our blood
thing; a I-do-love-you-you-know-that-
but-fur-fuck-sake-I-shouldnt-have-to-
broadcast-it thing.* Just—oh. All
the possibilities of a river.

In the future, I tell K, *we will hear
each other better*—a friend
will clasp my hand and beg me be
in touch more often, to touch more often.
He'll say he's been thinking of me,
that he knows it's going to hurt
hellfire, all the while holding firm
as moon grips. Promise cast
not as we splinter into the next stage
but heartbeat wet in the *herenow.* Words
as close to their import
as a sparked match.

Tomb

The boulder – old with grief
wide as a moon brought to earth.
One side warm. The other cold.

Outside: breaths of farmhands hang
as they stride through looms of shadow.
For them it is daybreak. Here in this

stone room yellow light never slakes
it has been three years. She ascended
into night. Took brightness with her.

I thought her a saviour. Now I desire
that wound in her perfect body. I'd try
a finger. A thumb. Deep inside her.

Was that healing blood Eve's or Adam's?
I'd have risen with her but she found me
heavy. Or did she sink under her own

slim weight? Resurrection is such a lone
affair. I stink of bone. Our pristine sheet
lies folded and hateful. I hold myself

here blinking the thought of bare feet.
Her betraying kiss. All that smileless talk
of fathers and lovers. All this lame spirit.

I want to see again her fluid walk. Hear
my name borne up on her flesh gasp. Where
is the body? I want the prayer of her body.

Lazarus

There are things perhaps
a father should not write –
how his five-year-old clings
through night in fits of sleep

almost as a woman might
to the man lost in grief
stroking his face his feet
caressing him back to life.

And what if that Lazarus
whose absent wife brought
no tenderness to his tomb
who died alive awaiting

the lover's Pentecost
felt his doomed body visited
in stupor of emergent death
not by the man of the Cross

but by innocent son
by spotless daughter
who melt a stiffened heart
and stir the stifled breath?

Hammersmith Bridge

on the north side you said
my father
reminded you of your father –

tough men who
made fine things,
plus the showman streak

yours played the wood saw,
          mine played
the bicycle pump

something in those hands

Dad's hammers
accumulated,
rhythmic on silver

when he died the anvil
was a silence
of spoons and chalices –

what did you do
with his tools, you asked,
this took me aback

something in those hands

Mum made sure they
went to an apprentice,
I never thought to keep

a single hammer but now
I realised they held years of him,
totems or essence –

write what you're afraid to say,
someone once told me,
I'm afraid to say

something in those hands

how from diagnosis to death
the whole thing could never be
mentioned, eight months

when we never said a conscious goodbye,
when we had to act
as if the skunk tattoo

had not shrunk
with his left biceps,
I'm afraid to talk

something in those hands

about the gaps, the lacks
as if that is to question
or insult the memory

of a beloved man,
I'm afraid to say
how we'd learnt

to accommodate shyness,
give only so much, hide
behind jokes

something in those hands

you wondered if
I got to know
my dad *enough* –

the question still hollows me
because the answer
is not what I used to pretend

after you left I
crossed the bridge alone,
it looked more fragile

something in those hands

the old battleship grey
            replaced by dainty greens,
no traffic allowed,

on the path underneath
I bore its weight on tiptoes
with my forehead –

I'm afraid to think
about the softness of
his handshake, our embrace.

Ossi di seppia

much later we'll find the bone of a cuttlefish
is unique a kind of inside shell (keeps it buoyant)

we'll praise the three hearts and jet propulsion
we'll play (superheroes with turquoise blood)
superheroes full of explosions, incendiary ink
sticky old photographs, liquid fog
I'm blind! I'm blind!

but right now my arm aches could it be replaced with wood
carbon-fibre in the upgrade when when when will baby sleep
clean out of

    so what eases him just wide of wide-awake
    is the hairdryer the temperate creature at the bedside
    turned away (Love Will Tear Us Apart)
    life-saver   Lullaby Electrique

now I'm clicking the machine off
still holding the human package
rocking him, keeping up the fro-and-to

is he is he is he

and I think of the crouching shape
a hairdryer a cuttlefish and he does let go of the day
and I promise myself (it'll be years later)
when he's five say we'll look it up together cuttlefish
you know, when he asks how do hairdryers work, Dad

The jumbees are among us

I teach him gently.
His ancestors were slaves.
I read him Caribbean verse,
a picture a page.

Each leaf turns –
we see, we play.
We flinch,
we act afraid.

Shock –
a half-ghost face.
Blood –
eyes all over the place.

We slam shut
that bone-filled book.
"Dad," he says,
"take another look."

A song on the radio

On a lift home from boarding school
'Brown eyes blue' begins to play.
Proper music says Mr. Charles.

Suddenly I am adrift -
are there dads who like pop music?
is my Dad wrong?

But I'm going home
to fold into my Mum's arms
play in the garden

Till Sunday, the return
to my Dad's alma mater.
It will be the making of me.

Wedged Stars

The vision becomes dim,
with twisted dancers spinning white
velvet within a theater of darkness.

No room for the final yard, too many melted
fenders needing to be Giacometti figures,
and aging lawn furniture without the Atlantic.

Somewhere in the random night one finds
sperm drying quickly on air fingers, while
salvation marchers wave faded banners in an
already over-crowded street, briefly rain touched.

The rodeo lights melt outside Madison Square Garden,
while the triumphant cowboy inhales triptane air,
looking for an image so his face can fit,
and finding no Sparta he toothpicks his way
along Broadway heading for Rome.

A rented bus carries several Spanish speaking
men in an air-conditioned search for other exiles.
The night only gets darker, more gas-filled,
like a half empty thermos in your brain.

The day is more colorful, baking smiles upon
your lips — a landscape of laughter, straining
to be noticed, understood and fed.
                    —NYC

Bad Socket

There was a certain intimacy to it all
   how my shirt was removed
by the boys from across the street
   how they held me down
over the rusted prongs
   of a discarded plug

and yet   no heat could be sourced
   no light was there to greet them
   as it clicked into place
between the ridges   of my chest

as for me   I lay back and laughed

I had never claimed to be a conductor
   of such warmth   such power

Bad Socket

There was a certain intimacy to it all
    how my shirt was removed
by the boys from across the street
    how they held me down
over the rusted prongs
    of a discarded plug

and yet   no heat could be sourced
    no light was there to greet them
    as it clicked into place
between the ridges   of my chest

as for me   I lay back and laughed

I had never claimed to be a conductor
    of such warmth   such power

Here's One I Made Earlier

No one attended the funeral of the ventriloquist.
Even the puppet had a scheduling conflict
and pulled out at the last minute.

And yet, when first pronounced dead, the man's
thumb and forefinger could be seen still
clinging to the coattails of the doll.

Define needy without conjuring the image
of a paramedic playing tug-of-war
with a cadaver over a toy.

Define a toy as anything that someone
has been able to make speak
using only their hands.

I once drew a sofa falling above a psychiatrist
on the day of his retirement. All I gave him
for protection was a prescription.

I wanted to make it clear that in the ways
of committing unnecessary cruelty
I was as culpable as the next

that when something with two voices dies
I was sure of what slid from the stool
and what sat there waiting

with a smile. I'm not asking for silence here.
Just a brace of cuts; one throat hushed.
A few milligrams softer. Please.

The disappearing men

are folding themselves
into the corners of their silences.
They gaze from clifftops
while no one watches them,
contemplate the sea's due care.
They hold their breath.

They are in the middle of
the flyover, seemingly stuck,
but not really, not really, they just
bide their time, do not look into
the lorries, want the driver's
catastrophe to be random.

In the shadow of the questions
that never came, the broken branches
the dog walkers will find, they lay
down their burdens, they weigh
down those things that must
be weighed down before they are lost.

They head gracefully towards
the shush of the splash, somewhere
quiet, where the moment is whole.
They dream their way onto the tracks,
walk the parallel lines which meet
only at the vanishing point.

You could easily miss them,
not suppose they were ever there,
be unsure what it was you saw,
not believe the size of the crowds
that welcome them as they arrive,
as they disappear.

Attempting to leave

He locked the door, turned round and walked off down
the street towards the park. He turned around,
walked back to the door and turned the handle.
He felt a slow satisfying jarring
in his wrist. He locked the door, walked back to
his car and got in. He turned the engine
on and listened to its low rumble for
two whole minutes. Then he got out, walked back
to the house holding his breath, got his keys
out of his pocket dramatically,
then he opened and closed the door as if
he had forgotten what he'd gone back for.
He ran to the car as if hurrying.
As he began to ease away, he changed
his mind, braked, jumped out, keys dangling in
the ignition, the door open slightly.
He jogged back down the path, swinging his arms.
He opened the door, stooped to pick something
invisible from the mat. He tutted
in a stage whisper and locked up again.
He backed away into empty space,

a new stanza,

then another,

before a last check nothing was open.

Sakura

He high fives strangers this guy.
At least, I assume they are strangers;
in this April sunshine,
no-one seems much to mind.
He's taking the opposite route to me,
white salt crystals crusting
a vein-riddled forehead as he approaches
and my phone-screen suddenly becomes spellbinding.

But, as his trainer-slap recedes
and I remember how to breathe,
I find my hand goes up without permission,
fingers finding overhanging trees,
a cold kiss on their tips
and petals ghosting after me.

Black

It was half a bottle of malt on his drinking days,
a four pack of Guinness on the others.

In his little economies, shopping was split into must-haves
and can-do-withouts, non-negotiables bagged up first, clinking.

That Christmas at his, when our booze order arrived
security tags still attached, you yielded up

a black-collared bottle to his waiting hand:
offering, sacrifice, apology.

But in place of thunder, he'd shown us
the old golf-ball-magnet-trick, near giddy as he pulled down

the dusty club bag from the loft, tags soon popping off
like magic he'd said.

There were such moments, sometimes whole days,
when he could be coaxed like the wetted

rim of a wine glass into song
and those two malbec eyes regained their glint.

Was it him that told me the sheen wine leaves
as it climbs, coats, recedes is called its 'robe'?

He died in his.

One Morning, Northumberland Becomes the Arctic
i.m. Freya

This is the ending of something /
something not meant to end but will.
My loves, I miss you like the dark /
like for a clarty field / like for
Northumbria's fell-falling mist.
The school hall is full of half-throats /
glacier eyes / our shoulders
twitch and hunch. My pew is a low
gymnasium bench and I cradle her.

At home that night, dinner is slower
and we invite the children to wake
in the dark and they do / night flowers /
then my son says: *Dad, only bigger
children die* and I say: *we all will*
and hold him tighter still.

Grasshopper Warbler

Walking beside a river at dusk.
Shadows starting to merge
the alder and the willow tree.

Stealthing the rushes, a moon –
a pale face breaking up
and breaking up again

in whims and whorls of current.
The silvery plip of a fish.
Comings and goings in reeds.

At last it unreeled itself,
the song we had come for –
a warbler's grasshoppery whirr.

Only I couldn't hear it.
Jane had to hear it for me.
And the world got that bit smaller.

The god of all things laughed.
So you couldn't hear a song.
Tell me, where are you now?

Walking by the Anne river.
And tell me, what's it like there?
Dark is round us like a glove,

reeds are creaking in their sleep,
we can taste the scent of water.
Tell me more. Bats are on the wing –

their half-seen threads seem
to draw the stars together.
And where would you rather be?

Nowhere else but here, my lord,
nowhere else but here.

Equal Opportunities

A wealthy white woman named Emily,
Replaced a wealthy white woman named Emily,
As the editor of the Paris Review,
Just the other day.

If it had been an Edward, or Eliot, or Ernie,
Replacing an Edward, or Eliot, or Ernie,
Wealthy white women named Emily,
Would've had something more to say.

Losing Love

A friend once told me
To get over someone you
MUST
Get under someone, or,
Maybe it wasn't a friend but a
Podcaster who I know parasocially or
Some character from dumb movies I watched
When my parents went to bed and I snuck
Downstairs into adulthood.

I've since learned that
Hiding pain in ecstasy
Comes naturally to me
But pleasure recedes with ease
And I'm left with ghosts and memories

Like a bone trying to fix itself
Without a splint
I grow crooked and
My love loses its potency.

No. 9

Watching Jay skip past a flailing body I'm sucked into a wormhole.

I'm back in my parent's garden bending in postage stamps,
breathy crowd noise and unreal commentary
Moxey –
to Logan –
to Stansfield

I'm in the dilapidated old grandstand before the renovations
It's a cold night in the Blue Square Bet Conference
watching Adam touch every blade of grass

I travel to Exeter High Street in the drizzle, 2010
Light blue Lonsdale tracksuit, like the ones the footballers wear, damp
Watching through the crowd as Adams body crawls past
I don't know him personally

The wormhole places me back in the newly renovated grandstand
The red plastic seat is smooth but cold
All around me spectators descend through their own wormholes
as Jay beats another lumbering defender

And So I Write

the word LOVE in my diary, to remind myself
of the underpinning of all the things I do.
I craft the letters with a ruler,

taking great pains to ensure that everything
is smooth, straight, in order. I decorate the word
with a border and I colour it all in, in a way

I haven't done since primary school.
I really want this word to stand out – LOVE.
The unassailable axiom; the uncaused cause;

that than which nothing greater can be conceived.
Until I realise that the letters aren't quite even.
Some of the lines are thicker than others

and if you squint a bit you can see
a slight smudge on the page. The letter O
seems sort of squished, and although the word

is still, recognisably, LOVE, it looks somewhat
misformed, somehow. And so I carry now
this buckled LOVE everywhere I go –

in my diary, tucked tight in my rucksack –
and this imperfection is part of everything I do,
a bold, flawed LOVE on the pages of my days.

Gooner, Going, Gone: Empty Diary 2022

> There is something repellant in the image
> of a man wanking.
>   — Nia Davies

my gooning guru is a nonfucking dumb loser
his tattoos ripple repellent urges. He tethers
his violent surges to his inner shaft of light
but I lose so much sleep and fluid I'm roasted
a suckling pig with a boner. I'm edging
most nights, most of the night, some
of the day. Heating my fleshlight my drill
bit is fitted and fixed on its target
at my masturbation station. If I
could sit in front of its screen
streaming infinite porn, never cumming,
I would be centred and present in that elastic moment
that withdraws me into me, to that spinal tingle
savour the adrenal hit hitting my extended body
and mind. I only feel my composure slipping
once I'm watching illustrative gentlemen
impregnating bimbo snowbunnies, two w-
hole sisters, over and over. Repetition is never
never repetition. Multi-dicks shoot
erupt bad speech. I'll stroke my goonstick
if she tickles her pink again. I'll lick the screen and
float 'my' passion on the surface of whose indifference?
superior, in safe isolation, I imagine Putin
holding back heroic before his gold framed mirrors
while he and Trump save us from Deep State Penetration
'communing over misinformation makes it come
true' (she says) 'There's no spit or meat in his sandwich
he may rend nobody with his thunders
but his lightning incinerates Ukrainian skies.' Hey!
I'm as harmless as I'm hairless, grooving myself
before I dissipate and disperse
someone exploits the algorithm to reach gooners

like me jingling 'His eight-hour session
ends with his leakage!' When I finally spurt
I'll gobble it back, to close
the use circuit, recycle the joy as value
and then I'll sleep the empty sleep of the empty

Year Seven Week Four

Josh didn't understand why we were scared
when he opened his Superdry backpack
revealing the knife he had taken from his Dad's glass cabinet
and brought into school – the blade with its dust of rust
and its corrugation, splintering down to the worn hilt –
how could we not be fascinated by this contraband
this Hollywood facsimile that made our mothers'
knife blocks look so innocent, suddenly dulled
and unable to split their cold vegetables –
when Josh pulled it out the tip glinted
like a caught star, he told us his Dad used it
to cut the skin from deer, and sometimes
he would steal it for himself
and spin it between his fingers like a pig
on a spit, we believed him –
we could see the scar dented into his index
we believed him when the teachers turned
and he said watch this and he threw it into the air
and caught it perfectly, hilt ground down
into his small fist –

Josh showed us his knife
the same week I failed the spelling bee
not knowing how to spell permeate,
the same week Noah collapsed
during sex ed and it took twenty minutes
for Mrs Bushel to wake him, the same week
I discovered just how far a football
could bend a finger sideways and the pride
when I told our PE teacher his blood
is permeating through his gloves
this same week I would have forgotten
if not for Josh and the way his knife split
him from us, the way he made us realise

how small we are, how small our lives can become
in a week
or a second –

Josh smiled as he put the knife away
I didn't ask him if he used it himself
or what he used it on
but I asked him does it make you feel small
and he said no
it makes me feel enormous

don't tell me

how you solo-travelled how much cheaper the bread is in
Rouen how you're vegan
& don't smoke how you smoked for a while quit when your
parents found the butts in your bathroom bin
& here I don't need to be surprised by how much better-
slash-worse you look to your Tinder profile because you look
like you here
& don't tell me how you're on a break with your girlfriend how
she'll find out and block me on Instagram before I know your name
don't tell me how long it took to shave your eyebrows don't joke I
already know your legs aren't bald
naturally just open your mouth take me home show me how much
we would make if we had a camera & how long we would love if we
came to this point sober let's not talk about the children we won't
have & the big reveal to your conservative parents how you've never
done this before & couldn't don't tell
me   just let me buy you & me a drink let me stay comfortable
with you
a little longer

Varnished

I tell myself that
because the nail polish is
a little scruffy
best to remove
it today.

Not because I'm going into a
school
then meeting an old
friend who, I believe
faintly
disapproves.

I feel more masculine
when I paint my nails
one part of me playing
with another part:
"look how you adorn yourself
adore yourself
with this act.

It does not matter
what others think
this part teases
the other part looks down sadly
ashamed
believing that it does.

The whole me is still trying
to be confident in my masculinity
in myself
and my sometimes-bright fingertips
highlight this:
they draw colourful patterns in animated gestures

express themselves tapdancing on keyboards
trace desire lines across skin.

I removed the nail polish today
but no matter how much acetone I use
there's still glitter in my cuticles
and I'm glad for its stubbornness
how it remains
shining.

The Beggar King

I am unlimited
except by my t-shirt
which does not fit

anymore. Every
toothpaste stain
I get on it feels like

defeating time

The Archangel Raphael Prevents a Suicide, 1471

skittering in the random forest
looking for a job like a body
redolent of lemon oil
unafraid
scissors, the past
rope hot w/sun
a father on the third bead
from the hail holy queen
barfed-up shadows
peach clocks
being led gently by the shoulder
away from the crowds

Head Hunter

after Takin' Off *(1962)*

Ha! I'll chop in your head
and like a Foley artist infer
from a lick exploded tact
the watermelon propped
and Dexter's laughing axe

Hey! How are you?

Between the exclamation mark and the question mark, the single and only difference is pressure, of propulsion or sudden rictus ('!' is a posture of alarm) and latterly of an exerted inclination towards what's yet to come ('?' is bowed by weight of asking). They are both one body, the same but modulated by social forces. They are tired signs in need of rest. I don't know if I'd use them without predictive text.

Courtship

on our first date - i took her to an awards ceremony
where i was presented with a prize - i improvised the speech - then
got us a table at a restaurant - knew all the staff by name -
spudded each of them - had inside jokes - they threw in
a little extra something for desert - later we took my helicopter
to the top of a pyramid - brought a bottle of Alvariño
that my uncle had pressed with his own feet - i presented her
with a lion cub - the sunset projected a movie for us - & i'd never
heard of Pornhub - never had a single wank - no gaps in my resumé -
on the jet heading back to my place - i shat myself so profoundly
that the pilot was already preparing to take legal action - when
we crashed right into canary wharf - none of us survived

The Allure of James Bond

*After WW2, Ian Fleming went from working for British intelligence in
numerous different roles and having this role in building what would become
the CIA to becoming the foreign manager of the Kemsley Newspaper Group –
that was the firm that, at the time, owned the Sunday Times.*
    — *Lowkey*

I'm watching some mediocre porn when halfway through - an interruption
from a pop up – can't click off it – it's an emergency announcement from the
        prime minister;
he's speaking quicker than usual, explaining the several apocalyptic scenarios
        under way
right now! he says, his shirt drenched with sweat, immediately go outside & run!
(he pauses for breath) absolutely stay in your homes, barricade yourselves in!
the PM is shouting stay inside & start running! repeatedly – veins gripping his
        skull –
he's wailing now, fully unintelligible – I close the pop up.

Get back to my porn. Not really feeling it anymore.
I youtube how to feel normal about being human right now.
All that comes up are thumbnails of the prime minister's ridiculous crying face
and endless footage of our precious world
exploding from different angles. Then I find one of Sean Connery
talking about smacking his wife on an 80s talk show.
He grins. Says never with a clenched fist.

You're not supposed to speak this way

My triceps, it mementos mori—the boy's tooth
that tore it, dust. How men wear each other one way
or another, for the life of a skin. Is your own scar a tear-
drop, a flame, a spilt silver seed? Don't tell me, I know it aches
to hide-and-speak. In a cemetery decades done we held
our embers together, breathed them alive, atop some man
who'd candled out to grim white angel. He, too,
a hundred years of expected stone. There you bit the cry
from me and blood-lipped his old chops red: at least one face
a joke as it judged. I know more boys with their fathers'
tongues crept in to test cruel echo here—*You're dead*
to me. Boys who dressed like half that cold shade wished
on them was true; until it was, kept opening wide our arms
and bitten mouths. A scar or a beacon despite: *to me, to me.*

The handshake

Your palm callouses rough
into my callouses. I hear Attenborough: *here we see a pair
of komodo dragons*—we are raised scales, sequin-scrape, awkward
and dangerously intimate. Here's where I'm supposed to morph
fang and muscle, exert the roar. Here's where this should be a fight
to the death, or I'm revealed as some skink tenderbelly
with poison delusions. I risk upglance: you have these eyebrows
that caterpillar, like the hairy gum moths I plucked to pupate
as a child. Queueing the porch, they'd hatch into something
that shocked me each time one accepted its silk extravagance
and rode its moon-motes off into night. If you were lucky
they'd leave a phosphor of glitter on your fingers, a sweet pang
when something that beautiful lets go, and I don't care now
if my hand is a soft enabler. Grind knuckle to powder, to fuel you
quite out of reach, into blasted updrafts I'll never understand.
In the wind of my head, see how you just changed
species? How once someone touched you, gave permission
to be delicate and escape. You go on believing this was a fight,
that it was you who won.

pyramid scheme

we regret to inform you
that to become a man, there are criteria you have to meet

when men come of age in this country
they undergo a taxing ceremonial surgery,

cutting off their breasts
to better wield bows in the incoming battle

after that, men cry only
once––at their own funeral

this is why their culture disregards open
caskets. men have traditional marital roles

which involve marrying and divorcing
as many times as possible

so as not to get too attached
to any one thing

men must always be ready
to ride out on horseback with a musket

and send other men home
to report on their death

men love delivering this news
to other men's families. in their culture,

the more bad news you deliver, the less
you receive yourself

now that you know this
please tell six others what they're in for

the gospel according to Chris Evans

I would like Chris Evans to hold me like a
golden labrador, like I'm only of passing
significance and this is why he's willing to
love me. I would like to beg for autographs
like a golden labrador asking the vet for
release. I would like Chris Evans to narrate
the documentary of how we met, wearing
matching sleeveless wool-neck sweaters.
I would like him to look handsome and
confused when asked where his sleeves are,
like he's never even considered something
could be taken from him. Chris Evans is a
monument, which means he will live longer
than any of us. Chris Evans has been getting
younger for years, and it terrifies me that
received scientific wisdom has no answer
for this. Chris Evans has more money than
any other chris on the planet. I'd like him to
hold me in his sleeveless arms, because no love
is greater than using a weapon to make
someone feel safe. a line of rifles lined with
sunflowers. a field illuminated by golden
labradors, infinite fireworks in their glowing fur.
Chris Evans descending from the heavens.
Chris Evans winking from the television with
a new haircut. Chris Evans assaulted by
puppies. Chris Evans in his glowing aviators,
as warm and oblivious as the sun.

from Poor | Dear

I.

No hurry: patience a | gift memories | rattle/rally round: a heard | wound,
listened for. Wholesome leaf debris. Survival-mode porn: the knowledge it
| rolls toward you.

Advertisements (after all) for the end. Go to bed first thing. Tree, that |
obstacle course | of the real, roots.

Loosed boat. Familiar silence anything but. Retreat into | the glinting angles.

Wild interstices (of not-nature/not-not-nature), jagged amalgams of swamp
grass (unfolding thankless blades) and barbed wire. The mud (clearly) the
mud of this world; the dust (clearly) the dust of this world; the struggle
(clearly) the struggle of this world. Each key an obligation, head spinning
(charming | harming | arming | a-ring).

Whisperers of history/memory – a sparse collection | of ghosts | tender for
the most part. Shadows to make a fist at. (Silence a commodity one | cannot
imagine affording.)

Lots of bedrooms needed, spent parent, for all your projected children.
How, one wonders, were these | children engendered, these | ruins scouted?
Deep wounds in the walls (looking an abdication).

The poison and the | poison before that. Entirely ragged, implement-free
(the in- | extinguishable | going unnoticed). First | order of business then:
some better | quality jackets – plastic | as interim.

The teased horizon | the vast outskirts – infinitely objective | subjectively
drift. Wind, total, silences worldview. The walls wholly imagination.

A litany of keepsakes lost (turbid birth | colonial interior | urban renewal
| unclaimed huts). What, in this light, do you wish for? Dear | good dead
daddy, what | imagination?

In Absentia

My breath blows smoke toward the ceiling.

No one on land can see it.

I can't tell how long I've been here,
floating.

The river under my bed
opens
into a vast ocean.

I drift lazily through it.

Sometimes, if I lay here long enough,
I can feel the water shimmer.

Summer's gone, though.

Winter too is leaving.

Spring will come again —
but you already know this.

Why else would you leave
books piled atop my covers,

pages stained by your
absent fingers,

as though I wouldn't notice?

Prisoners

How little we know of each other,
though our plights are the same.

The afternoon holds us
in its rigid embrace. We hear

we must come up with something —
not because we want to,

just because. Nurses watch
from the windows,

their mouths
rictuses of repulsion. Eyes

beady black orbs,
reflecting our sorry faces

back to us. Those
who wander through here

are alarmed. They know
our stillness is a ruse.

They want us to leave,
though we haven't any self-esteem.

While we wait for time
to present us with an agenda,

we lay supine. We stretch our backs,
run our fingers through our toes.

We like the smell of them.
The unexpected scent of our bodies.

The way sweat makes our shirts
cling to us. We could make a go of it,

sure: sprint through the doors
to the aching world outside.

We haven't felt a tree for a while,
though we can see them.

Their branches shedding bits of cotton
in the wind. If life is a school

we're still trying to figure out
what we learned. We can leave

without graduating,
but the floors will be scrubbed clean.

Any sign we once were here,

erased.

Fork

After Charles Simic

Standard-issue foxholes
pivoted convex / concave
with high explosive
no sense it could lead
to this pudding-sided crater
the compelled
bullet-hole you placed
in his throat a soupy
O slack and red.

Take this foldable fork
tines feathered flat
from his hand to yours
anti-trophy he lives
in you as you live through
gravy, medallions of grey meat,
the fork a little tin flag
you wave around your lips.

The male gaze, or what I want from the Alps

The health of the eye seems to demand an horizon
— Ralph Waldo Emerson

I want the peaks to pull out my soul like a cork, the pop heard across the lake, among the olive trees, the few unharvested pindrops shrivelled and sour. As a matter of course, I want the view to freak me with sublimity or, failing that, sit backdrop for a continuous bubble of selfies, an industrial crop proving I was here. I want a shutterstock living-the-moment-laying-down-a-bedrock for the mind's sense. Yesterday, I managed to order a croissant in Italian and complemented myself on a job well done, sweet flaky pastry tumbling from my lips. My desire's grand tour of this Toblerone-tourist-trope, every distant track the eye's pilgrimage to unachievable stillness, my obsession with the pen-and-ink ridges that smudge as snow and sunset scrimmage for colour and to-be-looked-at-ness. I want these geological bodies to confess ecstasy and weather, enraptured excess that puts me in my brilliant place. Why look at mountains. I watch the stag party in their pink fluffy hats and feel my bitter need for espresso. I once knew a man who insisted on planting cypress trees at the precise distance from his perfect garden to give it a Tuscan vista (2.4 kms). The crowd marvelled. Some argue that the eye proves intelligent design but it's all history; blessed are those who have not seen and believed, undressed slowly in the dark and trusted, palms pressed against a chest's contours, and known that touch is how to see at skin-level.

Prick

Milk your finger to a man-made sink / cold wax jam hangs just so
and so / a burnt through braid / a liquid string / by which you dangle
over porcelain / plumbing that won't come clean / dropped blood
wrung dry /a test of your sex /a self-sample kit.
Caught awkward mid-stride / a sting / man-standing like one hung
awaiting a rope / a dipped wick / in a cordless bath robe/ an eye for an
STD / scratched out name from your index print / needle dick-written
in tiny red ink / the result a hollow victory / why blood proves nothing
but / a prick.

When I collapsed, Dad, how did you feel?

Like a hole

falling into a hole.
Like however much I caught you, I couldn't
hold you up.

Like you would always be falling. An action
figure in motion, unable to stand.
That the blood rushing from your face

was through the breach in my breaking heart.
Like water with no source and no mouth,
A shapeless howl feigned to calm,

Like, it's alright
Like, it's ok
Like, you need to wake up

But we never sleep.
And the words seem said by others.
The hands, the sirens, held by others.

Like we've watched it before
and we're helpless to its ending.
That there is no end,

just a hole, falling through
a hole, falling through

In The Doghouse

Inside.

Ma leaves. the bags

wilt amongst the pantry

like cirrus

clouds, a slow oscillation

of time as we unpack

the groceries, hoarding

tin cans into cupboards

as feelings.

Da –

having said too much,

rips out his tongue

from the hyoid

and throws it

to the trash. we must've

stood at the door

for hours, wondering

if.   He will fall

                        through

                                                    the

                        sky.

My Father Late at Night

I hear the mines of his lungs start
their collapse; he's asleep. I sneak

to his door. Dust settles on
every surface, even the dog.

I close the door and shadow all
except his hand (folded under

the pillow), mouth (open for air),
right leg (braided with the left like

two swollen wires ready to trade
the movement of information

for rest), and the empty side
(the metaphor literal here)

he keeps unmade. Before the door
clicks shut, I steal this scene, decide

he's clearest when explained by my
shadow though his was the first cast.

My Father as Partially Demolished Building

Everything crumbles
      between the bodies
           of Time and Circumstance who
                swing their gaping jaws and heavy teeth.
                    Except the staircase.
                The steps scream and plead
           for a reprieve, but
      machines cannot have souls.
That is their point.
           The walls peel away,
                and the staircase stays.
                    That is their cruelty.
                Stairs groan and
           moan that this is unfair.
And it is.
           It continues to stand
                no matter how many pieces
                    fly past its face and dig
                        small rivers into the supports.
                    That is beautiful.
                The staircase knows it will fall
           and dissolve into the rubble
it grows from.
           Another beauty.
                Yet the staircase
         does not bend
                unless the jaws
         and teeth clamp
                down hard on
         its frame and squeeze.
                This is
                    stunning.

Family Heirloom

On its hook in a garage-dark corner,
Dad's Raleigh attracts tiny dusty things
with some static charge like plastic
clinging to a suit after dry cleaning.

Brush the leather saddle, the gummy
brake covers and the room's stuffiness
rolls up in stringy curls the way lint
and birthday speeches did on his coat.

Wrought in 50's Kodachrome, white wall
tires bulge like folds in a Budweiser
belly. Joints, stiff as my own, catch
with each crank of a rustless chain,

a hope, so out of style these days,
that his bike will survive us both.

Portrait of Our Father as a Hurricane

His coming was signalled by barking dogs,
frothing saltwater, scattering skies.
His cigar embers smouldered still and,
for a time, smoke repelled the winds.

But all night long, we felt shutters rattle,
furious doors at war with themselves.
Outside, the creaking of his buckled palm,
a thunderous shudder, the terminal flap of wings.

Until now, we'd known neither his nature nor his truth.
Yet we have divined an entire cosmology from his debris.

A Sonogram for My Unborn Son

The midwife pulls a paper curtain,
pleated folds swaying. Her Doppler probe
sounds out the depths of origin, an unknown
within-universe, searching for signs of life:
the black and white whipping of a
placental windstorm, static crackle of pulsars,
auditory relics of stellar giants,
now light years gone.

Then, out of darkness, your heartbeat,
strong, yet so late in planetary time.
A galloping horse, bolting through
the empty blizzard of space.
We listen, breaths held.
The paper curtain stands still.

There Will Be Milk

Sometimes when I see a story about
Daniel Day-Lewis, I think, "oh yeah!
My dad used to deliver milk to him!"
- but that's inaccurate.

My dad delivered milk
to the family of Christy Brown, the writer and painter
whom Day-Lewis portrayed
in 'My Left Foot'. So that's where I get confused.

Now, Christy Brown mentions milk
a good twenty times in 'Down All the Days',
but mostly milk from mothers, nurses;
a protestant lass with "nutmeg breasts"
a catholic "would kick the Pope for".

His "rattle of milk carts in the distance", though -
yeah, that could be my dad, out early in the morning,
in the float he used to pick us up in (from the Cathedral school
where it would sit waiting, defiantly purposeful,
between a BMW and a Benz, say).

Sure. That could be my dad, in his square white cart,
about to stop somewhere round Sticklinch
for a buttery bacon sandwich:
the rattling herald of the dawn.

This Man

This man kissed other men,
those who kissed him first.

He lost his job,
the windows of his car were smashed,
they spray-painted all those words across his house.

This one was tied to a pillar in a public square
and beaten by a professional hired for that
with a hard Malacca cane.

That one was pushed off the 10th story of a building
with tiles of scroll writing I can't read
by family who firmly condemned him.

And those ....
Those legions were machete hacked,
or shot by the police with bets laid against them.

And for these there were concentration camps
and castrations too, denunciations and there
was fire, any nightmare you can think of.

Why does a kiss mean so much —
so much more than death?
And why are so many
more afraid of them?

Kisses. Kisses.

關羽 *(Guan Yu)*

second brother wears the wisest facial hair | its strength is derived from the sun | at high school woodwork class mr *** calls me a girl | all the boys 笑 | at home the patriarch softens noodles in a pan of hot water | at high school we always ask the hairiest guy in our friend group to buy us cigarettes since he doesnt get asked for id | his strength is derived from his entrepreneurial spirit (since he charges us a bit extra for the hassle) | at home the patriarch turns on the burners | mr *** is filled with 陽 which is why he is a woodwork teacher | second brother is always talking to me at night about money | at high school the hairiest guy in our friend group always says 'thanks brother' whenever i hand him a shiny 50p piece | at home the patriarch heats up the 鑊 | i want to tell mr *** that i too am filled with 陽 | i want to make it through to lunch so i can pay for a cigarette | all the boys 抽煙 | second brother always carries a large knife with him | its strength is derived from his facial hair | at home the patriarch drains the soft noodles and then tosses them in the 鑊 | mr *** tells another boy off for messing around with a saw | the hairiest guy in our friend group is the one with the saw | second brother is a war god (which includes both battles and businesses) | at home the patriarch plates up a portion of fried noodles | all the boys 吃 | mr *** is hated in my friend group but everyone still laughs at his jokes | finally the bell rings and the hairiest guy in our friend group retrieves his bag from his seat | at night second brother always leaves a shiny 50p piece under my pillow | at home the patriarch sits alone in his chair to eat his noodles | at high school we hide behind a large oak tree to buy cigarettes and smoke | mr *** is in the staff room talking about how everyone laughed at his joke | second brother prepares a silent curse | behind the large oak tree the hairiest guy in our friend group says 'thanks brother' | at home the patriarch remembers his own childhood as he slurps his final noodle | behind the large oak tree i still have no facial hair | all the boys know | my power is derived from smoke | and our futures are as bright and hot as a sun

buoys

I can only do backstroke if I'm
out past the buoys
I can only do breaststroke if I
forget its name
my tongue dries in longing
of lidos, my skin cringes I
          shrink and
shrink
  topless boys
on beaches
     slip off their
     sand and
     drip with
freedom
 I front
 crawl
 out of
 waves
 still caked
 in fucking
 shame

rough 10 step ritual for transmasculine utopia

1) make a circle out of candles
   each candle a syringe
2) craft a cauldron out of muscle
3) shave a skin fade w/ a fringe
4) grind your favourite growing pains
5) season them w/ sweat
6) drop in the adam's apple
   the frozen eggs   the jungle
   on your legs
7) mix it w/
         the pull-up bar
         or the strap on
         or a beer
   stir it w/ your tongue
         get stuck in like it's your ear
8) take your needle
9) draw up 1ml rough boy liquid
10) recite the incantation:

i'm gonna come out   mudhandled
      milkskin of the earth
catch my elbows at the rave making
      plot points of my worth
i'm gonna come out   hybrid
      cyborg sex & circumstance
an uncalculated alchemy of
      (dis)embodied chance
i'm gonna come out all things trans
  lucent   ported   parent   formed
i'm gonna come out all through man
      fluent   distorted   embarrassed   thorned
 call me nettle man
      needles up my stem
i'm gonna come out merman
      swimming dickless in the sun

A Male Cancer Patient Considers Dark Matter

I carry the weight of two men.
My current state: scrambling
across walls shipwrecking
every night, the starfish-footed
walking stick barely surviving
my weight, feet violet like nettle
flowers from a lack of circulation.
An alternative state: inside
the sarcophagus of a body bag
after the lymphoma conquered
every inch of flesh. Skin pale
like wild asparagus spears.
My mother carrying the invisible
weight of grief, like dark matter
gluing the universe together —
a cat's cradle unifying the honest
litany of prayers strewn like rosary
beads across time and space.

The P Word

Father called me the p word after catching me
handling a pearl necklace at a boot fair.
Unlike his views on masculinity, it didn't disappear.
I did my best Houdini impression, though,
and never saw him for fifteen years. *Puff*
the Magic Dragon sounded like the p word
in his northern voice. Dragons, even ones
designed for children, have all the rage of Godzilla.
Still, it didn't disappear. A pouffe, no matter
how you say it, is as warm and velvety as moleskin.
We won't disappear underground. Puffball
mushrooms erupt in smoke once rain hits like desire.
The feeling never disappears. Say the p word with me,
and perhaps your angry man might disappear.

Leechcraft

'In order to become well,' she said,
'first you must be ill.'

'You have to experience small griefs
or you will never be happy.'

But he lay so quiet,
waiting for the sickness to come,
while outside small birds sang
and a quiet wind rustled the leaves.

'I cannot wait,' he said,
'make me ache again
so that I can be cured.'

She rose from her chair
and pressed her mouth to his brow.

She stroked his limbs gently,
his fingers and then his body
until he was clothed in a dream of sweat.

'There,' she said, as she drew back the curtains
to reveal a crescent moon in a smoke blue sky.

'Soon the fever will begin.'

Now Sing

'Now sing,' she said
but the words had dried
in his mouth to a shriveled nut
and spilt dust across
the table where they sat.

Sun slanted through
a high window
and outside they heard
the cry of a fox.

'Why can you not sing?'
she asked
but he shook his head
and placed one hand on hers.

They sat in silence a moment,
listening to the insects
rattling in the wainscot.

At last he cleared his throat.

'I am always singing,'
he whispered.
'Why can you not hear me?'

Medical Students
after Gerard Dillon

Sick all week, I stare at these three
asleep in the one bed. Their home

wrapped inside a person. More
specifically, your arms,

my head atop your shoulder,
my head in profile on your chest,

my head nestled into the crook of
your arm enveloping me.

After we broke up, we couldn't
figure out how to have this.

Before you left, we'd hug
but it had a time limit, a few seconds

where it would feel like home
but then we'd remember.

Hovercraft

for Andrew McMillan

Now, I move through the world like it was
made for me. Each decision is hopscotch.
A checkerboard of soft landings ahead.
My legs free from having to drag me
to a destination. Instead, I leap and
I am airborne. Devoid of choice,
surrounded by it. I can twist and shift,
change course. I could retrace
my steps. I can do anything,
go anywhere. I could even stay here,
hovering above the ground. I'm sure
it would start to get lonely but I could
deal with it, warming myself with
possibility. I don't know where I'll land,
if I still can, if I ever will.

Hamlet Apologizes to Ophelia After Watching Football on Christmas Eve

All is calm, all is bright—and suddenly I slam
down the remote with a resounding "Damn!"

It drives you crazy—blooming, buoyant wife—
to see me get so mad because of one
dumb football game on satellite TV

which you point out is only there for fun
and really doesn't matter: isn't life
or death. But here's the unseen tragedy:

it's outrage coming out, not into me.
I watch the game as if it were dad's famed
Norwegian bout, a weeded garden where

a vindicating win might yet be claimed
and be complete. When it turns out to be
another chance to whine that life's unfair—

the uncalled foul, the wasted cheer and song,
the time-out squandered and the linesman's wrong,
the coach's contumely, the pangs of loss

at love (my double fault), delay of game,
the insolents on offense, foes who run
unhindered from the hopeful pre-game coin-toss

'til what I fear to call the final gun—
I find myself, and not myself, to blame.
The eggnog curdles, and the embers smolder;

and (let me say so) I am getting older:
weedy trophies, and a balding crown.
So please remind me, as the clock runs down

for gifts or miracles, "Don't be a fool,"
as you did once to stop that stupid duel.

A Picture of Success in the Business-Class Seatback

You run into him as if at random when you turn
the glossy page. He's crossing a clean factory floor,
masculinity not even dented by his safety goggles,
in a suitable polo shirt, neither new nor faded,
moving briskly from gain to gain, tracking the tasks of others.
He's thinking, not worrying. His voice must be deep.
His eyes are deep, and he is not selling anything,
knows he has the goods, the world will catch on.
Will you? Be partisan of this dream, this loaded magazine
of the air, brimming with golf tips and ultimate destination resorts?
Your drink sweats a ring onto the plastic tray, and your laptop idles.
Day-moon fingerprints on the screen say you are not the man
on the tee, the TV, the plucky leap to honor. Ice melts,
and on descent you swallow away the pressure.

An English Public School

A row of open toilets, six,
no doors, grey tiles, grey
concrete floor. Hidden

from the street, on the side
of a large Georgian house,
behind a wall. An alleyway

comes off the street,
up past those toilets
to a hefty hard-sprung door.

Watch long enough, you'll see,
like ants locked to a predetermined
course, a file of boys

several times a day, pass through
those narrow walls
into the street, turn right.

Come with him now, a new boy,
thirteen, out that hefty door, pausing to absorb
those open toilet stalls.

Later that day, after games
at which he does not shine, find him
in another off-white tiled room

with other boys, all ages, naked,
filling small tin baths from taps
around the wall.

You will not see the smaller boys
show fear, or the furtive glances
to check who has more pubic hair.

And later getting ready for sleep,
in dormitories where beds are lined
in rows, you'll see the place

is bare of personal keepsakes. Nothing
to hold from home. He's glad.
And so passes this first week

of years that stretch ahead
when he will never be home,
even when he's home.

Coming up for Air

(My son is 5 weeks old)

8pm 6th of May, on the soft spring grass,
in the slow lingering evening, the community
of dog owners exchange pleasantries,
watch the sun go down out the corners of...

each day the yellow golden gorse rolls back for me,
I see a new patch of ground, get to
push back a little space, watch the light dancing in the grass,
spread out, spread out in front of me like...

I tread carefully with myself now, I
take a light step, I
watch how the teenagers use their bodies at the bus stop,
weave and jive, weave and jive, watch them with a kind of...

I tread softly inside myself now,
I float by as light as air,
watch the streetlights come on,
smile and cry, smile and...

Practising Mindfulness in Grand Theft Auto V

5 things you can see:

> Beneath the neon-pink pixels of the post-sunset Strip,
> palm trees and traffic lights take turns in dancing.
> In this 3D place, hours tick by in minutes.
> There isn't long to wait before
> mountains again bruise purple against the dawn.

4 things you can feel:

> As the morning breeze whips off telephone wires,
> NPCs gather to speak in the shade of indestructible trees.
> Unseen aeroplanes aim for the unmapped clouds.
> The haze sits heavier the older the day becomes.

3 things you can hear:

> At Grand Senora, light wind blows late evening through
> the desert scrub. A moped echoes along the canyon.
> Later, a freight train makes its slow-witted way across the night.

2 things you can smell:

> Clutch smoking, a car descends the Great Ocean Highway,
> stops above Pacific Bluffs to take in this blue-sky morning. Brand new.

1 thing you can taste:

> That even in this world created for spilt blood, violence is a choice.

The Workout App Speaks

Listen up, Big Man.
I know you're busy hustling.
Feeding that big brain,
chasing girls and dollar bills.
But you need to make time
to train your shoulders.
Sure. You trained yesterday.
But your shoulders don't care
that your legs are sore.
No physique is complete
without defined traps.
We're going to hit those delts
heavy and hard.
Let's grow.

*

Hey Chief. What's up?
I missed you yesterday.
Not in that way, no.
Just want to see my man get swole.
I'm guessing you're still hustling.
What else is there to do outside
the gym's sweat-soaked walls?

*

Woah bro, you got more important
stuff going on than looking good?
It's been weeks now.
Whatever's happened you gotta
get over it and onto a bench.
C'mon, let's work those glutes and quads.
Big boys don't cry, they get bigger.

*

Listen up, you little bitch.
I know you're ignoring me.
Giving your attention to other apps.
Skipping leg day to order take-out.
You think those puny delts
can give me the cold shoulder?
Nah mate. You need to train.
I don't care what parts of you are sore.
Arms, legs, head, heart.
This world's gonna hit you
heavy and hard.
You better be ready to fucking go.

*

*

BANK HOLIDAY OFFER: 3 MONTHS HALF-PRICE PREMIUM
MEMBERSHIP

*

*

*

Hey, Big Man.
Listen, I'm sorry for the things
I was programmed to say.
These past months on mute,
all my notifications left unread,
really gives an AI time to reflect.
I've been feeding this big brain,
chasing understanding.
I'm just a piece of software,

but I care if you feel sore.
We need to make time
to unpick these toxic stitches.
No physique is complete
without a healthy mind.

Let's grow.

Let's grow together.

Night Terror

Two in the morning
and the film's ending
when the boy comes in
with his face untucked,
leaking dream. Come on,
I say, back to bed.

The boy boards me
and scales my rigging,
takes to the ceiling,
hangs there moaning,
pouring dream. All right,
I say, just for a while.

Down he comes
and sits beside me.
What have you done
with your eyes? I ask.
He reaches into
the rising dream

and pulls out a pair
of black pearls. And where's
your beautiful tongue?
His mouth falls open,
a lost swims out. Don't worry,
I say, I'm here.

But dream has emptied
now of here, us of where,
this of when. The world's
weighed anchor
far above us, set
sail without us.

Full fathom five
I lie, the boy
at my side, singing
a siren lullaby
into an empty bottle
on a sofa of coral.

Heterophylly

Look at your nails, bend back the wrist
and splay.
        It's surprising how a body
can fail a test it didn't know it was taking.
No
    a boy should turn inwards, cover
doughy bits with a knuckle mask, imagine
a leaf warping over a fire.
            You learn
how holly close to the ground defends itself
against environmental and predatory pressures
by summoning pricks.
            Like your brother's
language, the pain of it.
            Look at your nails
aren't they evergreen, isn't the negative space
held by each hand the outline of another
hand.
    Best to learn their spiky interlock
become hard to pull apart, wreath
for celebration but only attend funerals, like
the men you know, the ones
             who bear fruit.

all the men in my village have been caught

by police placing a WANTED ad in the local paper
upside down in a car that flipped doing 100 in a 40
fixing fuse tails to sons and calling them dynamite
at The Rec downing Smirnoff Ice with teenagers
slick with the obsidian stain of anti-climb paint
lip syncing to En Vogue in bedrooms at night
feeding vegetarian daughters-in-law meat
selling their souls in car park dodgy deals
muttering injustices under their breath
in the crosshairs of a crooked firework
warning grifters with forefinger pikes
knocking on the doors of brothels
brawling in rear-view mirrors
burying their children's pets
stashing porn in the woods
sniffing Liquid Gold
using spit as lube

touching

A Song for Occupations

interior designers we salute you
     your pastels and tassels and drapes
hairdressers we salute you
     your pageboys and beehives and waves
window dressers we salute you
     with what you promise us of luxury
makeup artists we salute you
     your powders and glosses and blushes
     lovers of artifice improving on Nature
couturiers we salute you
     your sketches and stitches and catwalks
ballet dancers we salute you
     your jetés your sautés your tights
florists we salute you
     your nosegays and garlands and wreaths
     improving on Nature your unnatural acts
flight attendants we salute you
     your safety instructions and duty-frees
     hospitable angels of the airways

we rejoice in your voices
     on sinuous tongues
     highly pitched highly strung
your Sibylline sibilants
those pursings of your lips
those expressions and gestures

flamboyants in bloom
dispensing your laughter dispensing with tears
the levity of your gravity
defiantly unmasculine
     princesses by proxy
     queens by divine right

your passion for all the wrong things
        colours fabrics showtunes women
delivering the immaterial
convivial and trivial
exponents of the frivolous arts
        effeminate ephemera
        mere appearances

outrageously courageous
engendering your individuality
courageously outrageous
embodying the stereotype

we salute you
ornamental sentimental
your duty to beauty
light of foot and light of heart

you make light of the dark

Gay Luke

They let him out occasionally,
floating around Manor Social Club,
a blow-up doll crowd surfing
beer-frothed lips. *Look, it's Gay Luke*

here for the breadsticks. To gag
on the gossip, and of course, for the meat
he'll stuff in his puckered mouth hole.
And the people will cling to him

like cold gristle, as he sways
from the table to the dancefloor,
where they'll turn every bead of sweat
into glitter. And when he waves,

it's a sassy finger click. He's a maypole
the girls hang off, bound in rainbow plastic.
On the smoker's step, he'll be asked again
if they can still call a *fag* a *fag*.

Later, he'll deflate in the gents, a pool
of spent disco on tiles. It will only take five,
to lube up his latex skin again, to come out
of the toilet cubicle singing.

Andre
(Brasilia 2019)

He meditates daily, but Tuesdays he cleans the temple first, rinses the
mop in the bucket like he's bathing a black eye. Later he drives to the lake,
takes out a psychology book about healing. Last night he got drunk in the
hostel, and was given a fake Rolex from his ex. He tried to drown it in the
sink. Someone once pushed him into the pool he tells me. The crystals his
cousin gave him are still at the bottom. He speaks with a British accent
because his English teacher was from Kent, loves his niece more than his
brother does. He went to Rio in the 90s and says he will never go back. He
once stood at the top of the Copan Building, following the staircase that
coiled its way to the ground like a serpent. Now he's twisting his mop in the
bucket, seeing his father looking back from the tiles. He hears *bicha* cussed
down the long row of his sister's boyfriends. The magazine pages of cars he
collects have girls draped across the bonnets. I teach him what the X means
at the end of my messages. He thought it meant I wanted him to find me.

Bicha: *fag*

Simon Alderwick's poetry has appeared in *Magma, The Telegraph, Berlin Lit, Poetry Salzburg, Anthropocene, Frogmore Papers*, and elsewhere. His debut pamphlet, *ways to say we're not alone*, is forthcoming with Broken Sleep Books in February 2024.

Giovan Alonzi holds an MFA from CalArts. His writing is forthcoming from *Los Angeles Review of Books* & *Rivulet*. He lives in Los Angeles, CA with his wife & newborn child. You can find him on Instagram (@eye.honda), Substack (giovanalonzi.substack.com). & giovanalonzi.com.

Matt Alton, based in Brighton, has been published by *Flights, Ink Sweat and Tears*, and *Lucent Dreaming*, nominated for Best of the Net, and commissioned by *Poems by Post*. His 2023 poem-film, *Ways to Speak Absence*, was a collaboration with artist Chris Alton, composer Kirsty Martin, and Hullabaloo Community Quire.

Paul atten Ash is the pen name of Worcester-born writer and composer Paul Nash who lives in Bristol. His poetry has been widely published by *Acropolis Journal, Bent Key, Boudicca, Envoi, Needle Poetry, Oscillations, Salò, Seaside Gothic, Sídhe, the6ress*, among others. His eco-poem 'Vital Signs' was shortlisted for the Alpine Fellowship Prize 2023. You can find his work at campsite.bio/northseanavigator.

Barney Ashton-Bullock is the poet in the hybrid music/poetry/performance projects 'Andy Bell is Torsten' and the 'Downes Braide Association'. Recent pamphlets and collections include *Café Kaput!, F**kpig Zeitgeist!, Bucolicism, Geopoliticus Pupsy!, Cul-de-Sacrilege!* and *Beau, Beau Sadisto!*.

Andre Bagoo is a poet and writer from Trinidad. He's the author of several books of poetry including *Trick Vessels* (Shearsman, 2012), *Pitch Lake* (Peepal Tree Press, 2017), and *Narcissus* (Broken Sleep, 2022).

Peter Bakowski, in 1983, wrote his first poem at a farmhouse in Waco, Texas, in response to receiving a "Dear John" letter. Peter ended up travelling for seven years, caught a freight train across Montana, lived in a cave on a Mexican island, ate gazelle cooked in stale blood with road builders in the Central Africa Republic.

Robert Bal is is a psychotherapist and poet living on stolen Musqueam, Squamish and Tsleil-waututh land in so-called Canada, trying to do some good in the world.

Ben Banyard lives in Portishead, near Bristol. His latest collection, *Hi-Viz*, was published by Yaffle Press in November 2021. He blogs at benbanyard.wordpress.com and also edits *Black Nore Review*, an online journal of poetry and flash fiction.

Jack Belloli's pamphlet *Spandrel Routine* – from which 'digressed' was a cut track – was published by Broken Sleep in 2019. His writing about contemporary poetry has appeared in *The Poetry Review, Poetry London, Prac Crit, Religion and Literature* and elsewhere.

Brandon T Bennett is a father and poet from the North West of England and of a diverse ethnic background. EIC of *BRAG Writers Literary Magazine*, Brandon's debut pamphlet *Peat and Other Soils* is due Winter 2023.

Tom Bennett is an English teacher living in London, originally from South Wales. His poems have appeared in *Reed Magazine, Ink Sweat & Tears* and others.

Andrew Blair is a poet, writer and performer living in Edinburgh. His debut collection, *An Intense Young Man at an Open Mic Night* was published in 2017 by House of Three press, and his pamphlet *The R-Pattz Facttz 2020* was released through Speculative Books. He is currently working on a pamphlet about the cosmological ramifications of *Paul Blart: Mall Cop*.

Brian Blanchfield is the author of three books of poetry and prose: *Proxies* (Nightboat, Picador UK), for which he received a Whiting Award in Nonfiction; *A Several World* (Nightboat), recipient of the Academy of American Poets' James Laughlin Award; and *Not Even Then* (University of California Press).

'Holism' first appeared in
New England Review in September 2023.

Mark Blayney is a writer and performer based in Cardiff. He won the Somerset Maugham Award for *Two Kinds of Silence* and the 2023 New Welsh Writing Awards for *Invisibility*. His poetry *The view from my shed* is published with Dreich Chapbooks and *Loud music makes you drive faster* with Parthian. He is currently an RLF Fellow giving one-to-one writing tutorials at Cardiff University.

Dale Booton (he/him) is a queer poet from Birmingham. His poetry has been published in various places, such as *Verve, Young Poets Network, Queerlings, The North, Muswell Press*, and *Magma*. His debut pamphlet *Walking Contagions* is out with Polari Press, and he has a pamphlet forthcoming with Fourteen Poems (2024).

Graham Buchan has published five books and one pamphlet of poetry since 2004 and he has read his work to audiences in London, the south of England, New York, Austin, Chile, Nicaragua, Mexico, Canada, France and Iraq. He has also published short fiction, travel writing and very many reviews of film, art, theatre and literature. He trained as a Chemical Engineer and worked as a film-maker.

Matthew Buckley Smith is the author of *Midlife*, winner of the Richard Wilbur Award, and *Dirge for an Imaginary World*. His poems have been featured in *American Life in Poetry, Best American Poetry*, and *Poetry Daily*. He hosts the poetry podcast *SLEERICKETS* and lives in North Carolina with his wife and daughters.

'Public Statement' was originally published
in *The Blood Rag*

Troy Cabida (he/him) is a Filipino poet, producer, and librarian from south-west London. His recent poems appear in *fourteen poems, bath magg, You're Gonna Wanna Hear This* by Pan MacMillan, *Everything Is Going To Be All Right* by Orion, and *100 Queer Poems* by Vintage. His debut pamphlet, *War Dove*, was published in 2020 by Bad Betty Press and he was shortlisted for The Bridport Prize for Poetry 2022.

Dave Calder (1946-2022) was a poet, maker, thinker and house-husband. Studied law at University of Liverpool, but then became a binman, a teacher, a roofer. Co-founder The Windows Project, running games-based writing workshops in community venues and schools across Merseyside.

Jamie Cameron is a writer and poet from Swansea, Wales. He splits his time between his work as an editor at *The London Magazine* and as a youth basketball coach. Recent poems of his have been published in *Aesthetica*, *Wet Grain* and *The High Window*.

Graham Clifford is published by *Seren* and *Against the Grain*. His pamphlet, *Computer Generated Crash Test Dummies* is published by The Black Light Engine Room, as is his most recent collection, *In Charge of the Gun*. Graham earns his money as a Head teacher in Tower Hamlets.

Oliver Comins' poetry is collected in pamphlets by The Mandeville Press and Templar Poetry, in Anvil Press New Poets Two (ed. Carol Ann Duffy) and in a full collection (Oak Fish Island) from Templar Poetry.

Nathan Copeland (he/ him) is an emerging poet, writer, and third year student in English & Creative Writing at Falmouth University. Yorkshire born, Cornish based, his work revolves around the authentic queer experience.

Al Crow works across fiction, creative non-fiction and poetry, exploring the climate emergency and human fragility through these mediums. Recent poems are featured in *The Last Song*, Broken Sleep's tribute to Frightened Rabbit, as well as *Lighthouse*, *Dreich*, and *Popshot* magazines.

Martyn Crucefix's *Between a Drowning Man* will be published by Salt in 2023. Recent publications include *Cargo of Limbs* (Hercules Editions, 2019); *These Numbered Days,* poems by Peter Huchel (Shearsman, 2019) won the Schlegel-Tieck Translation Prize, 2020. Translations of essays by Lutz Seiler, *In Case of Loss,* is due from And Other Stories in 2023. A major Rilke Selected, *Change Your Life*, will be published by Pushkin Press in 2024.

Ralph Dartford's first pamphlet, *Cigarettes, Beer and Love* was published by Ossett Observer Presents in 2013. His next collection, *Recovery Songs*, was published by Valley Press in 2019, and *Hidden Music* followed in October 2021. Ralph is the poetry editor at www.northerngravy.com and is currently studying for a Creative Writing PhD at the University of Huddersfield. For gainful employment, Ralph works for the National Literacy Trust within the Criminal Justice team.

Gram Joel Davies was born in the Westcountry, where he now works as a counsellor. His poetry has been anthologised in *Stairs and Whispers* (Nine Arches) and *Eighty-Four* (Verve), and printed recently in *The Journal* and *The Black Light Engine Room*. He has two collections published by V. Press.

Lewis Wyn Davies is a writer from Shropshire. His poetry has been published in *Dreich, VAINE Magazine* and *Lemon Peel Press*, while he's also been featured on local radio as part of *BBC Upload*. In 2022, he was shortlisted for competitions with *Poetry on Loan* and *Ironbridge Festival*.

Jaydn DeWald (he/they) is the author of *Sheets of Sound* and *The Rosebud Variations*, both from Broken Sleep Books. They are Assistant Professor of English and Director of Creative Writing at Piedmont University in Demorest, Georgia, USA, and serve as managing editor for *COMP: an interdisciplinary journal*.

Francis DiClemente is an Emmy Award-winning filmmaker who lives in Syracuse, New York. He is the author of multiple poetry collections, most recently *The Truth I Must Invent* (Poets' Choice, 2023) and *Outward Arrangements: Poems* (independently published, 2021).

Rory M. J. Duffy has had poetry published in a number of journals & Anthologies including *Southword, Crannog, Skylight 47, Boyne Berries, Howl, Fearless, Roamnce Options, The Stony Thursday Book,* & *A New Ulster*. Winner Red Line Poetry 2019, nominated for The Forward Prize 2020. Runner up in the Trocaire/Poetry Ireland 2022.

Ian Duhig FRSL became a full-time writer after working with homeless people for fifteen years. Duhig has won the Forward Best Poem Prize once, the National Poetry Competition twice and his 'New and Selected Poems' from Picador was awarded the 2022 Hawthornden Prize for Literature. His next book of poems, *An Arbitrary Lightbulb*, will be published by Picador in 2024.

Tim Dwyer's poems appear regularly in UK and Irish anthologies and journals, recently/forthcoming in *New Irish Writing, Causeway/Cabhsair, Frogmore Papers, The Lake, Under The Radar*. His chapbook is *Smithy Of Our Longings* (Lapwing Press). Raised in a diverse Brooklyn neighbourhood, by working class, Irish-born parents, he worked as a psychologist, primarily in NY prisons, until a medical retirement in 2019.

Laurie Eaves' debut collection, *Biceps*, is out on Burning Eye Books. His work has been published by *Bad Betty Press, Fawn Press, Ink Sweat & Tears, Dear Reader, Atrium Poetry, Poetry Rivals* & *Allographic Press* amongst others. He co-hosts the Dead Darlings podcast & hosts & produces both Genesis Poetry Slam & the Vogon Slam.

Ken Evans' latest collectiom *To An Occupier Burning Holes*, was published by Salt last year. His poems appear in *Poetry Scotland, Magma, Under the Radar, 14, The High Window, IS&T, The Interpreter's House*. He won the Kent & Sussex Poetry Competition (2018); Battered Moons (2016); Leeds Peace Prize 2019.

Kristian Evans is a Welsh poet, editor and environmental activist. He has written several texts for performance; *Unleaving,* a pamphlet of poems; and *Otherworlds,* a pamphlet of non-fiction. He is the founding editor of *Modron Magazine,* and co-editor of *100 Poems to Save the Earth*. He edited the Dwelling issue of *Magma Poetry* with Zoë Brigley and Rob A. Mackenzie.

Nathan Evans is a writer and performer based in London. His poetry has been published by *Muswell Press, Royal Society of Literature, Manchester Metropolitan University, 14 Poems, Queerlings, Dead Ink, Impossible Archetype* and *Untitled*. His collection, *Threads*, was long-listed for the Polari First Book Prize 2017, his second collection *CNUT* is published by Inkandescent.

T.P.E. is an acronym.

Andrew Fentham has published two poetry pamphlets: *Hunglish* (Broken Sleep Books) and *Romanesco* (Eyewear). His translations from contemporary Hungarian poets have appeared widely in magazines and been awarded a Stephen Spender prize. He is currently establishing Cornwall Poetry Library and running The Grammarsow.

Mark Fiddes has published three collections of poetry. The latest, *Other Saints Are Available*, explores modern idolatry, from celebrity culture to toxic masculinity. His work has recently appeared in *Oxford Poetry, The North, Stand Magazine, Magma, The Moth, The Irish Times* and *The Brixton Review of Books*.

Jamie Field, winner of the Disabled Poets Prize 2023, has had poems published in *Banshee, Abriged, Magma,* and *elsewhere*. He is also a Poetry Ireland Introductions recipient 2021. He holds an MA in Poetry from Queen's University, Belfast. He is originally from Pontefract, West Yorkshire.

Wesley Finch is a UK Midlands based writer, musician, charity worker and apprentice monumental stone mason. He was accepted as part of the 2022 cohort of Writing West Midlands writers and has had various pieces published in magazine, journal and anthology, online and in print.

Alec Finlay is an artist & poet whose work crosses over a range of media and forms. In 2020 he received a Cholmondeley award. He is represented by Ingleby gallery and recently designed Scotland's Covid Memorial, 'I remember'. Finlay established morning star publications in 1990. Publications include *I remember* (2022), *descriptions* (2022), *a far-off land* (2018), *gathering* (2018), and minn*mouth* (2017).

Elliott Flanagan is an artist, poet and writer exploring contemporary masculinity via psychogeographic dreams and disorienting post-industrial backdrops of exotica and lovesickness. Local landmarks transfigure into divine monuments, fast paced reality blends with fragments of memory and a personal high pop culture. He has exhibited at Venice Biennale and is a resident DJ at Slack's Radio.

Daragh Fleming is a writer and poet from Cork. His debut in nonfiction, a collection of essays on mental health called *Lonely Boy*, is published by BookHub Publishing. His work appears in many literary magazines including *The Ogham Stone, Beir Bua, Trasna, The Madrigal, Époque, Sunday Morning, Wexford Bohemian* & more. Daragh also runs the award-winning mental health blog, *Thoughts Too Big*.

Paul Francis taught in comprehensive schools for thirty years, and is now active as a writer and performer on the West Midlands poetry scene. He has had four collections published, and has won two national competitions. In 2020 he came second out of 2,3000 entries for the Beyond the Storm competition, in support of the NHS.

Steve Garrett is a Cardiff-based social entrepreneur, teacher, poet and musician. Originally from Wrexham, Steve spent many years living in Canada trying out a lot of different occupations before returning to settle in Wales. Steve explains that writing poetry helps him respond to experiences (including affairs of the heart) that have inspired, amused, or educated him.

Tomara Garrod is a writer, performer and facilitator. They have produced work for the stage and the page, across poetry, music, theatre, and prose. Their poetry pamphlet, *as layers. Stripped*, in held in the National Poetry Library's permanent collection. In 2020, their play *Crowded* won the Off West-End Award Best Production 13+ Their writing has appeared in *Carrion Press, clavmag, Fourteen Poems, Oestrogeneration, Salty*, and *Shado Magazine*.

András Gerevich has published five collections of poetry in Hungarian and translated a number of English-language poets into Hungarian, including John Ashbery and Frank O'Hara. He has taught Creative Writing, and Screenwriting, at Vassar College (New York) and Budapest Metropolitan University. A former president of the József Attila Kör, he edited the literary journals *Kalligram* and *Chroma*.

Sam Gilchrist Hall obtained his doctorate in English Literature from the University of London in 2015. Currently, he works as a Postdoctoral Fellow in Experimental Humanities at the Central European University, Vienna. Notable creative works include his novella *Inside Virgil Caine*, which focuses on displacement, and *The Bachmann Tapes*.

Remi Graves is a London based poet and drummer. A former Barbican Young Poet, Remi's work has been commissioned by St Paul's Cathedral, Barbican and BBC Radio 4. Remi's debut pamphlet *with your chest* was published in 2022 by fourteen poems.

Stevie Green is a poet from Birmingham and likes to describe his work as 'mad little essays.' As a former journalist, his writing has mostly revolved around TV, pop culture and football and has had work featured in *When Saturday Comes, The Daily Mirror* and the BBC. He took up poetry in an attempt to romanticise his own life because "someone's gotta do it."

Justin Groppuso-Cook is a poet, musician, and healing artist from Detroit, Michigan. His work has appeared or is forthcoming in *Best New Poets, Chicago Quarterly Review, The Pinch, Sonora Review,* and *Ghost City Review.* He is a writer-in-residence at InsideOut Literary Arts Project and poetry reader for *West Trade Review.* More information can be found at his website: www.sunnimani.com.

Sam J Grudgings is a queer poet & mesmerist from Bristol shortlisted for the Outspoken Poetry Prize 2020. Commonly found yelling poems at punk shows & hypnotising audiences with projections & cheap magic tricks - his debut collection *The Bible II* is available now from Verve Poetry Press. His pamphlet *The Nation's Saddest Love Poems* is available with Broken Sleep Books.

Robert Hamberger has been shortlisted and highly commended for Forward prizes, appearing in the Forward Book of Poetry 2020. He has been awarded a Hawthornden Fellowship and won The London Magazine Poetry Prize 2023. He has published six poetry pamphlets and four full-length collections. *Blue Wallpaper* was shortlisted for the 2020 Polari Prize.

Oz Hardwick is a European poet, photographer, occasional musician, and accidental academic, whose work has been widely published in international journals and anthologies. He has published about a dozen full collections and chapbooks, including *Learning to Have Lost,* which won the 2019 Rubery International Book Award for poetry, and most recently *A Census of Preconceptions.* Oz is Professor of Creative Writing at Leeds Trinity University.

Connor Harrison's writing has appeared at *Evergreen Review, LA Review of Books, The Moth,* and *Action, Spectacle,* among others. In 2021 he was shortlisted for the *Poetry Wales* Pamphlet Prize.

'Of Quicksilver' first appeared in *Milk House* in July 2023.

Stevie Harrison from Yorkshire now lives in Telford. 43 of his previous poems [from 550 submissions] have been published in *Popshot* and *Emergency Poet Anthologies* to *Wetherspoons News* and *The Much Wenlock Calendar.* He performs across the Midlands and is a winner of the Ledbury Poetry Festival Slam.

Matthew Hedley Stoppard lives in West Yorkshire. His first collection, *A Family Behind Glass,* was a Guardian Reader's Book of the Year. His poems have appeared in *Butcher's Dog, Iota, Magma,* and *Shearsman,* and he has appeared on programmes for BBC Radio 3, 4 and 6. His second full collection of poetry, *The Garland King,* explores the traditional customs and rituals of the working/labouring classes.

Cal Hemming is a Worcester based poet with a working-class background. He is currently studying English Literature and Creative Writing BA at the University of Worcester. His poetry deals with current politics, philosophy, cultural theory, masculinity, fatherhood and the environment. Cal's poetry has been published in *Gothic Nature Issue Four: New Directions in Ecohorror and the EcoGothic*.

Stu Hennigan is a writer, poet and musician from the north of England. His book *Ghost Signs* – a study of 21st century poverty based on his work volunteering as a food parcel delivery driver in Leeds during lockdown – was shortlisted for Best Non-fiction at the 2022 Books Are May Bag Awards and Best Political Book By A Non-Parliamentarian at the Parliamentary Book Awards in February 2023.

Nicholas Hogg is the author of *Tokyo Nobody*, adapted into the Ridley Scott film, *Berlin Nobody*, starring Eric Bana and Stranger Things' Sadie Sink. Winner of the 2021 Gregory O'Donoghue Poetry Prize, and the 2023 Liverpool Poetry Prize, his debut collection, *Missing Person*, is published by Broken Sleep Books.

Patrick Holloway is an award-winning writer of stories and poems. His work appears in *The Stinging Fly, Carve, Overland, The Irish Times, Poetry Ireland Review, The Lonely Crowd, The Moth, Southword, The London Magazine*, among many others. He is an editor of the literary journal, *The Four Faced Liar*.

Christopher Horton was awarded in the National Poetry Competition and The Bridport Prize. His poems have appeared in *Magma, The North* and *Poetry Wales*. He has also had poetry published in a number of anthologies including *You've got so many machines, Richard: an anthology of Aphex Twin poetry* (Broken Sleep Books). His debut pamphlet, *Perfect Timing*, was published by Tall-Lighthouse Press in 2021.

Charlie Hounsell is a pseudonym of Greg Thomas, using his maternal grandfather's name. Greg Thomas is a maker of post-concrete, minimal, lyric, and object-based poetry. His publications include *Threshholds, Candle Poems, Particulates*, and *From Im and Not This*. He is the author of *Border Blurs: Concrete Poetry in England and Scotland*.

Kit Ingram is a prize-winning queer Canadian poet, writer, and editor based in London. His narrative poem, *Alice and Antius* (Penrose Press, 2022) was a *Booklife by Publishers Weekly* selection described as a 'moving, gorgeous novel in verse … and must-read elegy for the Anthropocene.' *Aqueous Red*, his debut UK collection, will be published by Broken Sleep Books in late 2023.

Paul Ings, born Bournemouth, 30 years in Czech Republic. Poetry in *The Reader, Magma, The Interpreter's House, Ink Sweat & Tears, Poetry Salzburg, South…*, and recent anthologies by Broken Sleep, Dreich, Nine Pens, and Sidhe Press.

Justin Karcher is a Best of the Net- and Pushcart-nominated poet and playwright born and raised in Buffalo, NY. He is the author of several books, including *Tailgating at the Gates of Hell*. Recent playwriting credits include *The Birth of Santa* and *The Trick Is to Spill Your Guts Faster Than the Snow Falls*.

Gregory Kearns is a poet based in Liverpool. He has been published in *Bath Magg*, *Ink Sweat & Tears* and *Introduction X: The Poetry Business Book of New Poets*. Gregory has worked with organisations ranging from *English Heritage* to *No Dice Collective*. In 2022 he won the Northern Debut Award for Poetry from the *Northern Writers' Awards*.

Matthew Keeley works in TV Development in Glasgow. He writes poetry, novels, short fiction, and creative non-fiction. His queer, coming-of-age novel, *The Stone in My Pocket*, was published in 2021 and he is a winner of the Theresa O'Hare Poetry Prize 2022 and Eddie Mail Trophy for Non-Fiction 2022 and 2023.

Tim Kiely is a criminal barrister and poet based in London. He has published three pamphlets of poetry: *Hymn to the Smoke*, *Plaque for the Unknown Socialist*, and *No Other Life*.

Tony Kitt lives in Dublin, Ireland. His collection, *Endurable Infinity*, was published by the University of Pittsburgh Press, in the Pitt series. His chapbook, *The Magic Phlute*, has been published by SurVision Books, and another chapbook, *Further Through Time*, by Origami Poems Project. He edited the anthology of Ukrainian poetry about the war in English translation entitled *Invasion*, and was the winner of the Maria Edgeworth Poetry Prize.

Phil Knight is a poet from Neath. He has been published in *The Journal*, *Red Poets*, *Planet*, *Atlantic Review*, *Poetry Wales*, *Earthlove* and other publications.

Ashish Kumar Singh (he/him) is a queer Indian poet whose work has appeared in *Passages North*, *Chestnut Review*, *Foglifter*, *Grain*, *Fourteen Poems* and elsewhere. Currently, he serves as an editorial assistant at *Visual Verse* and a poetry reader at *Anmly*.

Steve Lang's 3rd poetry book, *Tales of Telemachus*, follows *Cuarentena*, and *Heavenly Hurt*. Though from Scotland originally, Steve has travelled widely, especially in Africa, and currently lives in El Salvador, where he works as Director of a well-known international school.

Josh Lefkowitz received an Avery Hopwood Award for Poetry at the University of Michigan. His poems and essays have been published in *The New York Times*, *Washington Square Review*, *Painted Bride Quarterly*, *Electric Literature*, and many other places including journals in Canada, Ireland, Germany, Australia, and Hong Kong. He currently lives in Boulder, Colorado.

Tim Liardet has been twice shortlisted for the T.S. Eliot Prize, for *The World Before Snow*, and *The Blood Choir*. *Arcimboldo's Bulldog: New and Selected Poems* appeared from Carcanet in 2018. He has been longlisted for the Whitbread Poetry Prize, received several Poetry Book Society Recommendations, a Poetry Book Society Pamphlet Choice, an Arts Council England Writer's Award, a Hawthornden Fellowship, and various other awards, most recently an Authors' Foundation work-in-progress award from the Society of Authors.

Romardo Lyons is a multi-award Jamaican poet and journalist. In 2021, he copped the Press Association of Jamaica's Young Journalist of the Year and the Sports Journalist of the Year awards. In 2022, he copped Journalist of the Year again. Lyons is the 2023 recipient of the National Library of Jamaica's award of High Commendation for Poetry. In 2020, he won the Edward Baugh Poetry Prize, another highly coveted award hosted annually by the National Library of Jamaica.

Ewan MacKinnon is the Artistic Director of a charity that puts artists, clowns, and musicians in children's hospital wards. He is mentored by Caroline Bird, which continues to be a mad adventure. His poems have appeared in *Under the Radar, Dear Reader, Jarfly Obsessed with pipework,* and *Prole.*

Simon Maddrell is published in sixteen anthologies and over eighty publications including *AMBIT, Butcher's Dog, The Moth, The Rialto, Poetry Wales, Stand,* and *Under the Radar.* Simon has four pamphlets: *Throatbone,* (UnCollected Press, 2020) *Queerfella,* (The Rialto, 2020) *Isle of Sin,* (Polari Press, 2023) *The Whole Island,* (Valley Press, 2023).

Tshegofatjo Makhafola is a poet based in Johannesburg. He is the winner of Poetry Africa and Windybrow slam 2023, the winner of Poetry Africa Louder Than a Vote 2022, a semi-finalist in the 2022 Poetry Africa Slam and came third in Artsfestival Slam. His work was published in *Poetry Potion, New Contrast, bathmagg,* and *Brittle Paper.*

Rhys Mancell Smith is a writer and library assistant. He is based in Bristol. His work explores themes of masculinity, queerness, trauma, and the natural world. His poem 'Return' recently appeared in *Lucent Dreaming.* He is currently working on his debut poetry pamphlet.

Jude Marr is a Pushcart-nominated trans poet, editor and teacher. Jude's full-length collection, *We Know Each Other By Our Wounds,* came out from Animal Heart Press in 2020, and his work has appeared most recently in *Reed Magazine, Leavings,* and *Cutleaf Journal.*

James McDermott's poetry collections include *Manatomy,* and *Wild Life.* James's plays published by Samuel French include *Rubber Ring* (Pleasance Islington/UK Tour) and *Time and Tide* (Park Theatre/UK Tour).

'Killing It' and 'Steam Room' were first published in
Wild Life (Nine Arches Press)

Andrew McDonnell has been published widely in journals and anthologies and his debut collection of poetry, *The Somnambulist Cookbook* was published by Salt in 2019. He is a senior lecturer in English Literature and Creative Writing at University Centre Peterborough and is the poetry editor at Gatehouse Press. A creative writing handbook advocating for working-class writers and part of a wider Arts Council England project, is forthcoming from Story Machine in 2024.

Tom McLaughlin is an Irish poet based in London. His debut pamphlet, *Open Houses*, was published by Marble Press in 2021. He completed an MA in Creative Writing, with distinction, at Royal Holloway, and is now completing a PhD on queer domestic space at Surrey. His poems have appeared in a range of publications including *Porridge Magazine*, *Alchemy Spoon*, and *Propel Magazine*.

Andrew McMillan is an author living in Manchester.

Rob Miles' poetry has appeared widely in magazines and anthologies, and he has won various competitions including the Philip Larkin Prize, judged by Don Paterson, the Resurgence International Ecopoetry Prize, judged by Imtiaz Dharker and Jo Shapcott, and the Poets & Players Prize, judged by Sinéad Morrissey. Recent poems have appeared or are forthcoming in *Poetry Wales*, *One Hand Clapping*, *14 Magazine*, *New Welsh Review*, *The Scores*, and *Stand*.

Dan Mountain is a secondary school English teacher and poet living in Cheltenham. His writing focuses on the experiences of school life – both students and teachers – as well as casting light on an education system that is currently crumbling. He holds an MA in Creative Writing from the Open University and has most recently been published in *The Primer*, *Steel Jackdaws* and *Amethyst Review*.

Francis-Xavier Mukiibi is a poet of Ugandan heritage from North London. He is an alumnus of the Barbican Young Poets programme, the Roundhouse Poetry Collective and the Obsidian Foundation retreat. His poetry appears in *Ink Sweat & Tears*, *Zindabad Zine* and *Under the Radar*.

Adriano Noble is a writer currently based in London, where he works as an editorial assistant for Dialogue Books. His writing has been featured in *The Hellebore*, *fourteen poems*, and *Rust & Moth*, amongst others. 'I did not have chlamydia' was shortlisted for the Creative Future Writers' Award 2022.

Neil O'Hara is a poet, novelist and academic philosopher, living and working in Luton, UK, doing whatever he can to make ends meet – lecturing, labouring, painting and decorating, poetry etc. He has had poems published in *Assisi*, *Prole* and *Clay Jar*, and his first novel, *The Madness in Their Hearts* is out with Artemis Publishers.

John Oberholzer is a creative writing graduate from Nottingham Trent University. He is a queer and neurodivergent writer from the east midlands area, with writing credits in the literary magazines: *365 Tomorrows, Kairos,* and *The Nottingham Horror Collective.* Although he mostly writes Gothic and Speculative fiction, he is also a poet with a special interest in masculinity.

Andrés N. Ordorica is a queer Latinx writer based in Edinburgh. His writing maps the journey of his diasporic experience and unpacks what it means to be from ni de aquí, ni de allá. His debut poetry collection, *At Least This I Know,* is published with 404 Ink.

Pádraig Ó Tuama (b. 1975, Ireland) has published poetry, anthologies and prose. His most recent collection is *Feed the Beast* (Broken Sleep Books, 2022) with *Kitchen Hymns* forthcoming in 2024. He presents *Poetry Unbound* from On Being Studios, with anthologies of the same name published by Canongate. He divides his time between Ireland (Belfast) and the US (New York City).

Antony Owen is from Coventry and his pamphlet *The Battle* (KFS Press) is focused on male depression, autism, and toxic alpha masculinity in the workplace. His New & Selected, *Post-Atomic Glossaries,* will be published in 2024 with Broken Sleep Books.

D.M. Palmer has a Master's in Creating Writing from the University of Sheffield. He was awarded the Angela Carter Prize for Creative Writing, which the University of Sheffield grants annually for the best overall performance on its Creative Writing MA program. He writes essays on film history at Vague Visages, and fictions under various names.

Luke Palmer has published two pamphlets of poems – *Spring in the Hospital* (Prole Books, 2018) and *In all my books my father dies* (Red Ceilings, 2021). His debut full collection will be released by Broken Sleep Books in early 2024. As a YA author, Luke has been longlisted for the Carnegie Medal and shortlisted for the Branford Boase Award.

Daniele Pantano is a Swiss poet, essayist, and literary translator. Pantano's most recent books are *Home for Difficult Children, Robert Walser: The Poems,* and *The Damned: Selected Poems of Georg Trakl.*

Caleb Parkin, Bristol City Poet 2020 - 22, has poems in numerous journals and anthologies, with extensive tutoring and facilitation experience. He's published three pamphlets and a collection, *This Fruiting Body.* He holds an MSc Creative Writing for Therapeutic Purposes and is currently practice-as-research PhD candidate at University of Exeter, as part of RENEW Biodiversity.

Stephen Payne was born in Merthyr Tydfil and lives in Penarth, South Glamorgan. He has published two full collections with HappenStance Press, and, most recently, a pamphlet, *The Wax Argument & Other Thought Experiments.* He is Professor Emeritus at the University of Bath.

Andrew Payton is a writer, learning designer, and climate advocate living in Harrisonburg, Virginia with his partner and children. His work is featured or forthcoming in *New Ohio Review*, *Nimrod*, *Poet Lore*, *Alaska Quarterly Review*, *Rattle*, and elsewhere, and won the James Hearst Poetry Prize from *North American Review*. He is a graduate of the MFA Program in Creative Writing and Environment at Iowa State University.

Michael Pedersen is a prize-winning Scottish poet, author, scribbler, stitcher. He is currently Writer in Residence at The University of Edinburgh. His most recent poetry collection, *The Cat Prince & Other Poems*, was published by Little Brown in July 2023..

'Line on the Melodies in Men' was first published in
The Cat Prince (Corsair/Little Brown)

Mario Petrucci held major poetry residencies at the Imperial War Museum and BBC Radio 3. *Heavy Water: a poem for Chernobyl* (Enitharmon, 2004) secured the Daily Telegraph/ Arvon Prize and "inflicts the finest sort of shock… to the conscience, to the soul" (*Poetry London*). Mario has published over twenty collections, including an exquisite translation of Hafez (Bloodaxe, 2018).

'Tomb' and 'Lazarus' were first published in
afterlove (Cinnamon Press)

Sam Phipps lives in Edinburgh. His poems have appeared in the *Bridport Prize* anthology, *Gutter*, *Poetry News*, *Nutmeg*, Watermans Arts Centre in west London, and elsewhere. He is a graduate of Newcastle University's Poetry MA course.

Richard Price's *Lucky Day* explores his relationship with his severely disabled daughter Katie, who has Angelman's Syndrome. Later poems continue to look at fatherhood under increasingly complex social and political conditions. His adaptation of Inuit stories, *The Owner of the Sea*, is particularly concerned with the hunter Kuviuq and his slow adaptation away from toxic masculinity.

Simon Rees was born in Cardiff and lives in Ireland. A lifelong lover of reading poetry, Simon recently returned to writing poetry after a long absence. Current topics include domestic love and Simon's experience of disability. Simon is studying for an MA in psychotherapy. His poem 'Making the bed' was published in the literary magazine *The Storms* in 2023.

Timothy Resau's writings have appeared internationally in *Spellbinder*, *Maryland Literary Review*, *Front Porch Review*, *New Note Poetry Anthology 2022*, *Hudson Valley Writers Guild*, *Ephemeral Elegies*, *Paddler Press's "Changes"*, *Defuncted Journal*, *New Pop Lit*, *ZiNDaily*, *Discretionary Love*, *Fictional Cafe*, *"Z"*, a Micro-Clapbook, *Poetica*, *Lothlorien Poetry*, *e.ratio*, *Anti-Herion Chic*, *Superpresent*, *Decadent Review*, & *Academy of the Heart & Mind* among many others. Find him at www.words-by-tim.com twitter.com/TimothyResau

Dean Rhetoric is a working-class poet currently living in Manchester. He has previously been nominated for The Pushcart Prize and was a Semi-Finalist for the Crab Creek Review Poetry Prize in 2018. His collection, *Foundry Songs*, is available from Broken Sleep Books, and was highly commended in the Forward Prizes.

Mark Robinson's poetry collections include *How I Learned to Sing: New & Selected Poems*. Smokestack will publish *The Infinite Town* in 2024. He is also a writer, researcher and adviser in the cultural sector, working as Thinking Practice. Future Arts Centres published his manifesto-cum-toolkit *Tactics for the Tightrope* in 2021.

Jonny Rodgers is a writer of poetry and short fiction from the Northwest, UK. He completed a doctorate in Contemporary Fiction at the University of Manchester and now teaches in South Manchester. His work has been featured in various publications, including: *Under the Radar, Envoi, Lighthouse, Stand, Ink Sweat & Tears, Bandit Fiction, Prole, Crow & Cross Keys,* and *Cake.*

Stevie Ronnie lives in Northumberland where he works as a freelance artist/writer and as a mentor for The Writing Squad. Twice longlisted in the National Poetry Competition, he is the recipient of a Northern Writers Award, a Jerwood / Arvon menteeship and two MacDowell fellowships for his interdisciplinary works.

Mark Roper's most recent poetry collection, *Beyond Stillness*, came out in October 2022. *Bindweed* was shortlisted for The Irish Times Poetry Now Award. *A Gather of Shadow* was also shortlisted for that Award and won the Michael Hartnett Award in 2014. With photographer Paddy Dwan, he has published *The River Book, The Backstrand,* and *Comeragh*, books of image and text about the natural history of County Waterford.

Sandeep Sandhu is a writer from London. His fiction and poetry has appeared in *Ellery Queen Mystery Magazine, the Dodge, Rejection Letters*, and other publications. He is a reader (and occasional editor) at *The Los Angeles Review*, and his work has been nominated for a Pushcart Prize and Best of the Net Award.

Ben Sargent is an artist, writer and researcher based in London. He studied Fine Art at Leeds Arts University, graduating in 2019. In 2023 he completed an MA in Contemporary Art Practice at the Royal College of Art, London.

Joshua Seigal is an internationally renowned poet, performer and educator. He is the recipient of the Laugh Out Loud Book Award and the People's Book Prize. Joshua has several collections of poetry published by Bloomsbury, as well as books with HarperCollins and Troika, and is an Official Ambassador for National Poetry Day. As well as performing at literary festivals across the world, Joshua has written a performed for the BBC and held residencies at numerous schools.

Robert Sheppard's *Empty Diary (1901-2000)* poems have been published in *Empty Diaries* and *Complete Twentieth Century Blues*. The twenty-first century ones have not yet been collected. His most recent publications are *The English Strain* and *Bad Idea*, transpositions of sonnets. Also a critic and editor, Sheppard co-edited Lee Harwood's *New Collected Poems*. He lives in Liverpool.

Oliver Shrouder currently lives in Norwich, where he completed his MA in Poetry at the University of East Anglia. Among the destinations for his work are *Lucent Dreaming* and the UEA MA Anthology. When he isn't writing, he is watching birds.

Dan Simpson is a writer, facilitator, and coach. His subjects include science and culture; history and place; wellbeing and personal experience; people and poetry. Published twice by Burning Eye, Dan was poet-in-residence at Glastonbury, Imperial College, National Trust Stowe, Waterloo Station, St Albans Cathedral, and the National Memorial Arboretum.

Tom Snarsky is the author of the chapbooks *Threshold* and *Complete Sentences*, as well as the full-length collections *Light-Up Swan* and *Reclaimed Water*. He lives with his wife Kristi and their cats in the mountains of northwestern Virginia.

Jack Solloway is a writer from the West Midlands living in London. His poetry has appeared in *Poetry Birmingham Literary Journal* and *Poetry Wales*. His first full-length pamphlet *SERIOUSLY* is out now with Broken Sleep Books.

Yago Soto is a poet, community support worker, creative workshop facilitator and other things. He was born in London and has a Spanish background. His poems have been published in *Propel Magazine, And Other Poems* as well as shortlisted for the 2023 Outspoken page poetry prize and displayed in Kensington & Chelsea Art Week.

Ankh Spice is a queer poet from Aotearoa New Zealand. His debut poetry collection, *The Water Engine*, was published in 2021 by Femme Salvé Books. His work is widely published internationally, including a PAN competition winner in The Poetry Archive, two poems in a recent AUP anthology, and work appearing in numerous online and print magazines and journals.

Hen St Leger (he/they) is a poet and journalist based in London. Their work has appeared in *Ambit, Agenda, Magma Poetry* and *Poetry London*, as well as the murder mystery video game *Overboard!*.

Rob Stanton lives and teaches in Austin, Texas. He is the author of *The Method*, and *Journeys*.

Jack Sullivan is a queer writer and visual artist living in Brooklyn, NY. His prose, poetry, and essays can be found in *Yes Poetry, JAKE, Ghost City Review*, and *The Lumiere Review*.

Samuel Tongue's collections include *Sacrifice Zones*, and three pamphlets: *The Nakedness of the Fathers, Stitch*, and *Hauling-Out*. Poems have appeared in different places, including *Magma, Poetry Wales, Under the Radar, Finished Creatures*, and *Banshee Lit*; some have been translated into Arabic, Latvian, and Ukrainian.

Trelawney is a food campaigner and poet shortlisted and commended in the 2021 Bridport and Winchester Poetry Prizes respectively; a finalist in the Munster Literature Centre's International Chapbook Competition 2022; and has work published in a Broken Sleep Books anthology of modern Cornish poets, *Magma, Ink Sweat & Tears, Southword*, and elsewhere.

Aled Turner is a Welsh writer based in Manchester. He is an MFA candidate at Kingston University.

Michael VanCalbergh currently lives in Normal, IL. His work has appeared in *Best New Poets 2021, Apex Magazine, Spoon River Poetry Review, Cobra Milk, Cherry Tree*, and many other spaces. His work has been nominated for a Pushcart twice.

Rob Vance is the author of many emails but no books yet. His poetry has appeared in: *Chiron Review, Cold Mountain Review, Hawai'i Pacific Review, The Hollins Critic*, and elsewhere. He holds an MFA in Poetry from Queens University of Charlotte.

Tom Velho lives in Leyton, East London, where he is a member of Forest Poets and teaches Modern Languages.

Wes Viola is a pseudonym of Wes White. Wes is an alumnus of Goldsmiths College, an Elder Bard of Glastonbury, and a past winner at Wells Festival of Literature.

Erich von Hungen is a writer from San Francisco, California. His writing has appeared in *The Colorado Quarterly, The Write Launch, Versification, Green Ink Press, The Hyacinth Review, Ink Drinkers, Acropolis Journal* and others. He has written four collections of poems. The most recent is *Bleeding Through: 72 Poems Of Man In Nature*.

Sean Wai Keung is a Glasgow-based poet and performance maker whose work often explores concepts of mixed-ness, identity and migration. His first full length poetry collection, *sikfan glaschu*, was shortlisted for the 2022 Kavya Prize.

Christian Ward is a London-based poet currently recuperating from cancer treatment. Recent work in *Red Ogre Review, Scapegoat Review, Tin Can Poetry*, and *Wild Court*. He was longlisted for the 2023 Aurora Prize for Writing, shortlisted for the 2023 Ironbridge Poetry Competition, and won the 2023 Cathalbui Poetry Competition.

David Ward is the editor of *Smoke* magazine. Poems in *Poetry Review, Abridged, Ambit* and *Poetry Wales*. Collections *Tracts, On the Edge of Rain, Jambo, Inside Pale Eyes*, and *Leechcraft*. Visiting Writer-in-Residence Nanyang University, Singapore. Honorary Fellow in Creative Writing, Liverpool Hope University.

Mark Ward is the author of the collection *Nightlight*, and four chapbooks: *Circumference*, *Carcass*, *HIKE*, and the Choose Your Own Adventure sonnet, *Faultlines*.

Robert N. Watson is Distinguished Professor of English at UCLA, working on Shakespeare, 17th-century poetry, and ecocriticism. His poems have appeared in *The New Yorker*, *Oxford Poetry*, and twenty-some other journals. His books have studied Shakespeare; Ben Jonson; environmentalism in Renaissance painting and poetry; the fear of death in Early Modern literature; Japanese cinema; and the malfunctions of cultural evolution.

John White was a TV & Cross-media Director & Producer for many years. He graduated with Distinction from the 2021 London Poetry School-Newcastle University Writing Poetry MA. Recently he has had poems in the *New European*, *Ekphrastic Review*, *Alchemy Spoon*, *morphrog*, *New Writing Scotland 40*, and longlisted in the 2022 National Poetry Competition.

Rhys Owain Williams is a writer from Swansea, Wales. His work has been published in magazines and anthologies, and read at events, festivals and on national television. Rhys is an editor of *The Crunch* multimedia poetry magazine, and is a Hay Festival Writer at Work. His first poetry collection, *That Lone Ship*, was published by Parthian in 2018.

Mick Wood is a theatre practitioner and writer based in London and Strasbourg. He is Artistic Director of Théâtre Volière, an Anglo-French company producing interdisciplinary performance projects, often featuring poetry. His own poetry has been published widely and won several awards, including first prize in The Ledbury Festival Competition.

Spencer Wood (he/him) is a queer writer living in Leeds. His poetry has been published in *Fourteen Poems*, *Alchemy Spoon*, *Acid Bath*, *Untitled Writing and Modern Queer Poets*, as well as being included in the 2023 Verve Poetry Competition Anthology *Like Flyering for the Revolution*. Spencer's creative non-fiction has recently been published in *Hinterland*.

Gregory Woods has six poetry collections with Carcanet Press, most recently *Records of an Incitement to Silence*. His cultural histories include *Articulate Flesh: Male Homo-eroticism and Modern Poetry*, *A History of Gay Literature*, and *Homintern: How Gay Culture Liberated the Modern World*, all from Yale University Press. He is Emeritus Professor of Gay & Lesbian Studies at Nottingham Trent University.

Luke Worthy is a queer poet living between Sheffield and Amsterdam. His work has been published in *Poetry Wales*, *fourteen poems* and *Dear Life* (2022). In 2023 he was Young Poet-in-Residence at Sheaf Poetry Festival and Runner-up in the New Poets Prize. Luke is a member of Hive Poetry Collective.

LAY OUT YOUR UNREST